Vertical Tutoring

by

Peter Barnard

Grosvenor House

This book is published by
Grosvenor House Publishing Ltd
28-30 High Street, Guildford, Surrey, GU1 3HY.
www.grosvenorhousepublishing.co.uk

A CIP record for this book
is available from the British Library

ISBN 978-1-907652-03-5

Notes on...Vertical Tutoring

∞ Teacher quality is not the problem; a system that undermines teaching and learning, is

∞ Centralism creates factory schools; progress is an illusion

∞ Schools create 'back-office' bureaucracies and close down 'front office' learning processes

∞ Centralism killed schools and schools killed the tutor: it is this that has disabled schools

∞ There has never been a time when every child has mattered less than now

∞ There is no parent partnership worthy of the name in UK schools

∞ Most training, including the NPQH, is about compliance to a system that doesn't work

∞ While schools have a culture of dependency, there can be no transformation

∞ To make progress, schools have to appreciate the nature of chaos and spiritual intelligence

∞ Year-based school systems don't work, have never worked and cannot be made to work

This book is a contribution to school improvement. It explores school management and Learning Relationships within a systems thinking framework. The book openly promotes Vertical Tutoring as the key to school transformation.

Peter Barnard is a former Headteacher of two large and very successful secondary schools and now runs his own consultancy on school improvement and (especially) Vertical Tutoring. He can usually be contacted either on his allotment or travelling the world watching hard-core punk rock bands! His website is www.verticaltutoring.org

ALSO BY PETER BARNARD

Chaos, Culture and Third Millennium Schools (2000)

Acknowledgements

Many thanks to Lesley Kennedy, my sister-in-law, who checked early drafts for error and did not charge me a penny: any faults that remain are mine: I no longer have a PA and am exposed to my original laziness and incompetence. Can I also thank Richard Clarke of Apocalypse Press who took my first draft and rightly reduced it by half. Richard did the same with my first book! The advice of Ralph Tabberer also remained critical; get rid of all the political angst and deliver the message of VT. I have no doubt that his important work at the former DCFS diluted the excesses of government during the first decade of the new millennium and that schools have much to thank him for. Ralph also advised that I look again at the work of Jonathan Haidt, teacher and writer, and this caused me to rewrite key sections of this book. Tribute must be paid to Nikki Knight, now a successful Headteacher in Surrey, and Roger Freeman, now retired. Nikki inspired the early fundamentals of Vertical Tutoring in its modern form, and worked with Roger on data systems to underpin learning conversations and parent/student alliances. Their support to me and their contribution to VT in the UK cannot be underestimated. Thanks too, to the other outstanding teachers of The Winston Churchill School in Surrey who (some decades ago) allowed a rookie Head to take a big risk or two with systems and learning as a process. I also need to thank the outstanding staff and governors of Sharnbrook Upper School for *going VT* and for creating a school of such unbelievable quality. I have no doubt that they will soon choose to be an Academy. John Clemence (now Principal), Ginnie, Hugh, Peter, Val, Howard, Kirk et al, remain inspirational in their passion and belief that only the best will do. It has been my good fortune to be part of two such great schools.
I need to return to Jonathan Haidt whose brilliant concept of *'the elephant and the rider'* in his book 'The Happiness Hypothesis' allowed me to more fully understand schools, learning relationships and learning as process; the key cultural elements of VT. Thanks must also go to the many, many schools that have invited me to journey with them on the road to VT. Finally, I must thank Patricia, my partner of some 30 years, and Laurent, my son. Laurent featured at the end of my last book when he was approaching 'A' levels and dreaming of being a rock star. Patricia has achieved her goal of designing gardens at the Chelsea Flower Show and Laurent has travelled the world with his hard-core punk band Gallows. What else do you do with a degree in English? Not surprisingly, I cling to my allotment and my 18 year old cat, Smudge, for my *quantum of silence.*

Contents

Preface

At the turn of the Millennium, I was inspired to write 'Chaos, Culture and Third Millennium Schools'. It used metaphor, Systems Thinking and common sense to try and explain why our inspirational schools seem to be so organisationally stuck. That was then. In 2010, we arrive at the start of a new epoch. A visionary new leader, Barack Obama, has become president of the USA and a new coalition government is in place in the UK. The world is in economic turmoil. Our backs are to the wall and things are set to get worse before they get better. Chaos has escaped and has returned to our organisations and to our culture: but there can be no better time to take stock, to review and plan new pathways: it is time again for new paradigms and direction.

For education, it is time to re-map the territory, put back the signposts, gather energy, and talk again of heroes and epic journeys. It is also time to develop policy and advise politicians before civil servants, think tanks, dodgy research and consultants confuse them even more. Indeed, our tired schools are very fortunate to have survived a decade of centralist waste, ideology and hypocrisy. The facts are simple. We seem to underachieve as a nation; our systems undergo constant tinkering and shoring up; there has been immense government waste and increasing interference in every aspect of our lives. Governments rarely fully deliver on promises and inequality remains rampant, in part because public systems are coping systems and not good at dealing with variation, adaptation and predicting outcomes. They cannot transform. Not only can we not afford the grandiose systems we have but the public systems themselves do not respond well to repair, and especially where the most vulnerable are concerned. For ideologies, the end justifies the means. At the base where the nurse, policeman, teacher and social worker engage with the public, all is not as it should be; there is uncertainty, fear and collateral damage and the wrong people are blamed when things go inevitably awry. Our new government has much rapid learning to do in order to build a more equal partnership with schools. At the same time the apron strings must be cut and reformed accountability established.

In our schools, signposts change overnight, direction is confused and the journey of our schools remains precarious. Schools follow their target scores instead of their values and this endangers the human spirit and what our schools need to do and be. We wrongly believe that teachers can mend a broken society by teaching repair programmes; meanwhile we fail to understand *Learning Relationships* and have forgotten how they work. Indeed, every school in the Land conspired to kill the lowly form tutor indicating a mass misunderstanding of management and leadership; in key areas, our schools can no longer distinguish good management practice from bad.

This is not the fault of teachers but of a system of compliance, regulation, bureaucracy and dependency in which they are persuaded to operate. There has never been a time when every child and every teacher has mattered less.

This book is a rambling attempt to arrest my teacher heroes from their lemming-like existence and show schools there is a better way. There is no real pretence at research, academic rigour or much else that resembles a book on education. In fact, after serving 38 years, half as a Headteacher, I still have no idea what education is and that is my good fortune. However, I do know what it takes to run great schools and I do understand how creative and high value people like teachers work best. Having done all of the jobs mentioned in this book and spoken to thousands who still do, it allows an insight or two.

Introduction

This book is a contribution to school improvement and is dedicated to schools. It explores the world of school organisation through the lens of Systems Thinking and explains why Vertical Tutoring offers solutions to the challenges facing today's schools. The book examines the link between centralism and school management and seeks to explain why there is almost a complete absence of innovation and transformation in our schools although schools and governments wrongly think there is. The book explores schools at an operational level and the confused assumptions surrounding '*education*'; school management and learning. Finally, the book attempts to explain the critical link between the school as an organisation and the development of '*learning relationships*' and in particular the fragile role of tutors, tutees and parents. **There is a critical reappraisal of how schools are organised and it unashamedly states that horizontal (Year) systems have not only long passed their sell-by date but have never worked properly and cannot be made to work to support teaching and learning. In fact, centralism and year systems combine to form a major destructive force that disables the school from building in higher quality teaching and learning. The future is vertical.**

This book is a kind of journey. It maps the route to Vertical Tutoring and explains why so many schools are anxious to explore and implement a complete change of culture to build new organisational systems based upon substantive *learning relationships* (how small loyalty groups and individuals support learning). We can take this to mean that Heads rightly want their schools back and VT will ensure this is so; politicians should delight in this because only then can they help. But even here there are dangers to be avoided. Old culture and orthodoxies have a habit of clinging on, and schools continue to make avoidable management errors as they implement Vertical Tutoring. The poverty of training and the absence of a theory of learning reveal unintended dysfunctional management behaviour in our schools. This is not the fault of Headteachers but of a system that prevents good people from understanding what it is to run a values driven school as opposed to one that is target driven.

In particular, this book proposes that the formal and singular one-size fits-all means by which schools are expected to resolve issues of social cohesion (PSHE, SEAL, Citizenship, assemblies) are deeply flawed and cannot work unless schools reconsider and reconstitute social and learning management structures (process). Hopefully all of this will become clear; **learning relationships before learning.**

I am told that people rarely read whole books anymore. Some dip into chapters and others read the last chapter first: teachers have asked me to include a little repetition in each chapter to help this process. A good friend, Ralph Tabberer, said I should reverse the book's order and concentrate on the message rather than theory. I have tried to do just that and consigned much of the management theory and personal rage against politicians to the bin. PGCE students tell me they don't read at all (too busy preparing lessons!) but just find the '*good bits*' they want '*for quotes*'. Finally I must apologise. In revealing a few of the paradoxes that beset education, I fully realise how easy it is for this book to become one such paradox. In highlighting some of the problems of prescription and regulation, this book prescribes the changes (VT) that thinking schools should make and which many are now making. However, good people and school leaders will realise this ambivalence and simply barge on through.

PAB
04/2010

IT'S THE SYSTEM, STUPID

The Guy In The Glass

When you get what you want in your struggle for pelf,
And the world makes you King for a day,
Then go to the mirror and look at yourself,
And see what that guy has to say.

For it isn't your Father or Mother or Wife,
Who judgement upon you must pass.
The feller whose verdict counts most in your life
Is the guy staring back from the glass.

He's the feller to please, never mind all the rest,
For he's with you clear up to the end,
And you've passed your most dangerous, difficult test
If the guy in the glass is your friend.

You may be like Jack Horner and "chisel" a plum,
And think you're a wonderful guy,
But the man in the glass says you're only a bum
If you can't look him straight in the eye.

You can fool the whole world down the pathway of years,
And get pats on the back as you pass,
But your final reward will be heartaches and tears
If you've cheated the guy in the glass.

Dale Wimbrow: 1934.

This poem was distributed to the English Cricket Team with good results although some seem to have lost their copy. Here it is dedicated to all who work in schools but especially to our teachers who try so hard to make an almost unworkable system work.

Chapter 1: Introduction: Systems Thinking and Vertical Tutoring

Managers talk about getting rid of deadwood, but there are only two possible explanations of why the deadwood exists: 1) You hired deadwood in the first place, or 2) you hired live wood, and then you killed it... W. Edwards Deming

There is a problem with this first chapter. It rambles, challenges and rages more than first chapters should. I would rewrite it had I time. We all get old! The challenge of explaining Vertical Tutoring (VT) is that it is inherently transformational. VT changes school management, builds value in, simplifies policies, improves social relationships and revitalises learning relationships. It brings back the sense of fun and achievement that centralist government policies and endless prescription have so badly damaged.

Understanding Vertical Tutoring (VT) at a conceptual level is relatively easy; understanding how VT works as a **learning process** within a school improvement programme requires a slightly deeper understanding: transforming to a culture of VT is also relatively simple but requires a re-examination of how learning as a human, organisational process actually works rather than how schools assume it works. Schools have all the right values; the problem is that these values are not translated into effective working practices; in fact, schools wrongly believe they are values driven when it is perfectly clear that they are target driven. Values will always lead to greater success than targets ever will. In effect, we have to understand why the organisational practices of schools don't work as expected and why schools do the things they do in the name of good practice. To effect a cultural change to VT requires schools to make a clean break with current organisational ideas and especially with year based organisational systems.

Understanding why schools do not work as well as they should is essential because this prevents schools as organisations reinventing management ideas that don't work as a learning process. To implement VT successfully means leaving behind virtually everything that we have learned about how schools as organisations operate. This can be exceptionally challenging for LTs (Leadership Teams) who have done so much to make schools work as well as they do. It can hurt. But why consider VT at all? The reasons lie deep in our schools where school improvement stalls again and again; when they stall as they inevitably do, governments leap into the vacuum and make things worse, or at best try to bodge things up with a little reform here and a little more inspection there. Unless we know why this is, schools will not improve as they should let alone transform as they must.

To change a school culture means confronting orthodoxy head on. Normal processes of consultation, training and organisational refinement, especially stemming from increased government regulation, do not work. Otherwise, schools as organisations will continue to make slow progress; they often plateau and organisational transformation does not take place. In fact, transformation within a year system cannot take place.

Politicians see teachers and school leadership as both the problem and the answer; a kind of personnel and training issue. Nevertheless, whatever centralist intervention is made, whatever the 'reform', the system seems to stall again and again. It seems that we have a western cultural problem in our schools, and politicians have no answers; indeed, such intervention has prevented schools from developing as organisations. Policy actions actually do more harm than good. In the US, Linda Nathan (2010) identifies similar conditions to those that exist in the UK. She describes the culture in US schools as one of endless initiatives intended to both improve outcomes and to allocate blame when initiatives don't work as expected. The title of her book is well chosen: *'The Hardest Questions Aren't on the Test.'*

And that's the problem. The school improvement effort needs to be focused elsewhere, deep in the school where the students first meets their personal tutors, where learning as a process should begin and where learning relationships first form. It is precisely here, on entry to our schools, where learning as a supported process begins and it is here that our schools make the biggest system management mistakes of all and trigger a whole series of practices based upon huge assumptions. Get the first critical part of the system wrong and the rest can never work properly.

Quite simply, there is a problem at the heart of school improvement. Having tried so many initiatives, having introduced so many regulations and having produced so much research, why is it that school education as a system is not working as it should? Why are levels of stress so high, teachers so exhausted, outcomes so unpredictable? Why is raising standards so difficult; challenging behaviour so bad? Why aren't we seeing any real change and why are school leadership and our excellent teachers so often rendered ineffectual? Why is this so, when those working in our schools are so dedicated and amazing and how does Vertical Tutoring seem to throw new light on our schools? Hopefully, the answers will become clear as we re-examine the learning relationships that underpin learning in schools.

Vertical Tutoring and Systems Thinking

VT at its most fundamental level involves a mixed-age approach (vertical rather than horizontal) to supporting learning as the key to raising standards and for providing the platform for better schools, better outcomes, better learning and a better society. In simple terms, instead of having horizontal, year-based tutor groups, we have mixed-age vertical tutor groups. Later, these will develop into full vertical learning systems. (Ironically, they already are!) But how is it that such a simple concept has within it the capacity to provide solutions to the big organisational, system and learning challenges that face schools? How could we miss something so simple and so obvious, something with so much pedigree and history; and so misunderstood? It is a UK thing. We come up with brilliant ideas and then throw them away. There is nothing in VT that does not go back in time.

For schools, the change to VT is a **cultural** change (or should be); it is not just a change to the pastoral system and those schools that think it is have not transformed. It affects the way everyone works and every policy and process in the school (or should do). Such a change should be both an evolutionary and revolutionary process but to make this psychological and cultural shift requires that we confront and counter the deep seated factory management and leadership orthodoxy that has dogged schools as organisations throughout much of the C 20th and which threatens to persist throughout the C 21st. Those schools that think VT is some kind of limited *pastoral change* are very wrong and their Leadership Teams (LT) should not be running schools.

For such a simple idea as VT, the capacity for schools to make a mess of such a change is unusually high and this is what is happening nationwide. Schools claim otherwise (as ever). This is not the fault of schools but of a system that has stopped or prevented managerial Systems Thinking. This book sets out why VT is such a powerful change agent, how VT raises standards and aspiration, why it is the base for improved teaching and learning and why we need to understand Systems Thinking more than we do. *Systems Thinking* demands that we first understand what is wrong because this will prevent reinvention of the past. This can make Systems Thinking very challenging to *successful* schools and especially *successful* Headteachers.

The 'F' Word

Let's make a start à la Gordon Ramsay. The 'F' word here stands for *Freedom*! It is not possible to work well, creatively and with joy without understanding what it is you have to do, and without the autonomy to do it well. OK. Deep breath...

First, strip away the fatty skin of unwanted ideology such as *Every Child Matters, No Child Left Behind, entitlements* and *Breadth and Balance*. Cut away all regulation and boil off the residue of inappropriate inspection. Remove all targets, Key Stages and the 14-19 curriculum and bin them. Ditch the unworkable and unpalatable recipes of endless *reforms*. Sever all school policies, procedures and practices and sear them with a blow torch. Chop appraisal into bits and feed it the birds. Keep reducing regulation until left with the rich stock of staff, students, parents and someone sensible from the Local Authority (LA). Shut parents in the school hall and don't allow them out until they decide *what matters*. Once done, you have 20 minutes (we have now left the "*The 'F' Word*" and joined *'Ready Steady Cook'*) to create a better school without using any of the previous ingredients, now discarded. This is your our best chance of understanding VT and building a VT culture. If you do not want to throw away the regulation, central initiatives and ideological preferences currently in play and think you can't possibly do better, you are probably suffering from an overdose of institutionalisation and should avoid schools and school management and stick to governmental recipe books.

Any teachers reading this should feel better already.

Systems Thinking: Making Work, *Work*

Having spent my 'retirement' working with almost 200 secondary schools, you notice things. The first is that schools are all trying to operate the same systems. There is almost no real difference between schools in the way they operate. On rare occasions, success is the result of exceptional leadership (maverick traits rather than organisational); on most occasions, any success depends upon the degree to which students are willing to comply and submit to school management and leadership behaviours. The second thing you notice is that all who work in our schools work incredibly hard. The third thing is that school managers have brand new job titles despite still doing exactly the same jobs! The fourth thing you notice is that everyone is doing the wrong job. Finally, you notice that schools sense that these observations are so, but have not quite been able to work out how they got to be where they are and how to innovate themselves to a better place. It is a management problem.

There is a long and interesting history to 'Systems Thinking' as a method for making work, work. Schools have always conducted *system reviews* and questionnaires but at a very superficial, low impact level. Questionnaires rarely work, as systems thinkers know. As far as I know, schools have never really been subject to a *Systems Thinking* approach; if they had, it would be unlikely that schools would be operating in the way they do within a larger system so beset by the strange and weighty catch-all regulation needed to make education appear to work. *Systems Thinking* should identify what is wrong, assess what is needed (better process) and initiate an improvement plan by identifying levers for transformation (Fig. 1). It has been interesting to see some Academy Principals working with expensive business consultants on school management and school set-up strategies (how I started out to learn Headship). Most end up with a slightly more efficient factory model but with grander titles for managers. The classic consultative approach to change (part of my own NCSL training) needs considerable caution when dealing with VT: such an approach can pander to the *'Headteacher's vision'* which is likely to be the same as all other Headteacher visions, when what it should do is talk the hard talk of values and Systems Thinking. Without a deep knowledge of VT any normal *consultative* approach tends to perpetuate old culture and treats VT as simply another *'reform'* among a government litany of so many failed reforms.

For our schools, *Systems Thinking* can be uncomfortable and challenging; it starts by questioning very simple operational practices that seem at first sight to be eminently sensible and regarded as *'high quality'*. Schools are not as straightforward as they seem. These are outlined throughout this book. Systems Thinking causes school managers to confront all sorts of demons few of which are of their own making. Today, schools are required to operate within an ever changing and hyper-complex web of so-called joined up safeguarding relationships that are close to unworkable. Ultimately, the change process to VT is one of liberation from such complexity. One Head described a session on Systems Thinking with her Leadership Team as *'brutal but necessary'. Moi, brutal?* Others simply see it as fun and *see* their schools afresh for the first time. Systems Thinking can feel challenging when the practice of decades is slowly taken apart and shown to be false, unworkable and damaging; this process of *unlearning* can be emotionally very dissociative so care is needed to reassemble working and learning relationships following any dismantlement.

However, the systems analysis that comes from Systems Thinking is the only hard part of the road to VT and is the route taken by this book. Unless we first understand and appreciate what is wrong in our schools, schools will never understand how to implement a better learning process that is values driven and more sensitive to and supportive of, learning. Systems Thinking simply reunites a school with its values and puts it back in touch with its redefined core purposes (what matters) by seeing learning as a joined up process rather than one fragmented and subject to a stream of unworkable government interventions, fixes and reforms.

VT ensures that *every child actually does matter* in a real rather than the dangerous, unworkable and ideological sense we now have. VT also ensures that every teacher matters which is also the opposite of the system we now have. Teachers are not the problem, a system that actually undermines teaching and learning, is.

The Systems Thinking Model

The simple process set out below (Fig. 1) needs outside expertise which is why so many schools that *go vertical* fall so short of what is needed. They assume they understand VT just as they assume they understand learning as a process and treat it superficially; they then end up reinventing the past. Such a process leads to *management by assumption* which is all too prevalent in schools and this is the direct opposite of Systems Thinking.

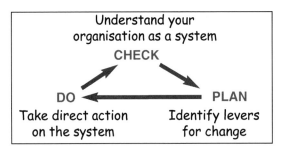

Figure 1: Systems Thinking Model

The diagram presented above is from the 'Vanguard Systems Thinking' website and is reproduced here with permission. It is an old model that has stood the test of time. This is what schools think they do via their SEF (School Evaluation form), parent surveys, student voice and feedback mechanisms but none of these really informs Systems Thinking and all are more likely to prevent substantive change. If Systems Thinking was better understood, most schools would not be working in the way they do.

For schools the purpose of Systems Thinking is to produce a more coherent learning process, to allow more organisational and individual freedom to think and innovate and to bring back what W. Edwards Deming called 'joy in work' (Neave 2000). This is done by inviting schools to look again at the way their organisations operate but this time through the eyes of process participants, especially students, parents, tutors, teachers and schools managers. Even here, great caution is needed. Schools wrongly think this is what they already do. Again, and despite their claims, they are wrong.

Command and Control v Systems Thinking

To move forward it is helpful to understand the different ways of doing things (Table 1) and once understood, learn to leave one behind (despite its near complete invasion of schools) and work on the other. We will not change the preferred government management style (Ideological and controlling, disguised as reforming) but schools can do far more to influence policy and have more control than they think as they start to move towards VT. Schools need to help politicians make better choices by teaching them how schools operate and that to do this VT is essential.

Table 1: Systems Thinking (Adapted from Vanguard Consulting Ltd.)

Process Focus	Command and Control	Systems Thinking
Perspective	Top-down (DCSF)	Outside–in (then inside out)
Design	Functional Specialism	Demand, Value, Flow (integrated process)
Decision Making	Separated from Work	Integrated with work (all learners and teachers)
Measures	Cost, output, standards	Related to purpose, capability and variation
Motivation	Extrinsic (target driven)	Intrinsic
Management Ethic	Manage Budgets & People	Acts on System (Improve learning process)
Attitude to Customers	Contractual	What Matters (produce great kids citizens/learners)

Politicians and the DCSF, not schools, remain the single most damaging cause of poor teaching and learning because they run the system they inadvertently undermine. This is not their wish but it is their karma. Deming put system faults as 94% belonging to the system builders (government) and only 6% to those trying to make the system work (teachers). Clearly, Ofsted is inspecting the wrong people!

In such a system (LHS above), all innovation and change is directed from the centre and this breaks all Systems Thinking logic, causing the Law of Opposite Intentions and the Law of Assumptions to come into play. In effect, Heads are not really running our schools as a learning process but are implementing compliance directives; this is a tragedy because I think the hundreds of Headteachers and LTs that it has been my good fortune to meet, would be very good at it given the chance. It is essential that the people best placed to do the work (the teachers and Headteachers et al) actually do the work, not politicians.

I do not want to get into a line by line explanation of Table 1, but simply offer it as a background theme and part of the explanation for the slow rate of school improvement.

Attention, however, should be drawn to the *'Management Ethic'* line in the Table above because contained here is one very big paradox! Schools are all about building *'learning relationships';* school managers naturally and wrongly assume they should manage people because they believe that people are responsible when things go wrong (this is what governments think). People get things wrong when the systems in which they operate are mal-formed and don't function properly. The first task of managers is to ensure that schools have an effective learning process and this process starts long before the students enter the classroom, not just after. Managers should first and foremost impact on **the process** of learning and this is the bit schools have made a real mess of for decades. The management function is to make the school system work as an effective learning process so that all involved can perform optimally. This is fundamental to any understanding of VT. Teaching and learning cannot improve at the rate needed in the system we currently use and we are falling behind as a country.
The challenges outweigh the capacity of the system to respond.

When people have real control over what they do and fully understand their jobs and the how the system process works, they perform better and are far happier and healthier. **At present, schools perceive they are in control but this is an illusion: they are certainly made to feel responsible when things go wrong: that is the trick!**

You learn much about tricks in a circus. Things go round in circles and the clown has a sad face.

Chapter 2: Year Systems Undermine Teaching and Learning

Where we are in our schools is C20th and where we need to be is C21st. Alongside the many successes of our education *system* there is considerable failure. Schools are delightfully simple. We send our kids there knowing that they will be safe and looked after by some of the most talented and dedicated people in the country. We are very fortunate. Children get taught, exams are passed and the process starts all over. On the surface, schools are very happy, well ordered places where people work extremely hard; they are to be admired for their achievements and the day to day miracles each performs. Not a word written here is a criticism of them although some might erroneously think differently.

From a Systems Thinking perspective, however, all is not what it seems. In the hundreds of schools it has been my privilege to work with, Headteachers want to improve their school for teachers and learners but find it difficult to pin down system blockages. Discussions with LTs lead to the following conclusions every time.

1. **All who work in schools are impressive people: the vast majority are absolutely the right people in the right place at the right time doing the wrong job**
2. **There is no parent partnership worthy of the name in English secondary schools despite the claims of schools to the contrary**
3. **Despite massive system intervention and centralist prescription, there has never been any successful school 'transformation' in England. There is a tremendous rate of change but nothing has actually changed at all. Most things go round in circles, sometimes backwards**
4. **Schools do not understand what it is to really 'care' even when Ofsted judges the school's pastoral system to be outstanding. Schools don't really 'care' but want to**
5. **'Waste' in schools systems is high: waste in the bigger DCSF system is colossal**
6. **Schools cannot innovate. The handful that can, have. Only maverick Heads innovate; risk-taking needs courage**
7. **There is no CPD (Continuing Professional Development) in our schools. The NPQH does not *'open minds'* as claimed. It tends to ensure compliance to a system that does not hold. CPD increases system dependency**
8. **Year-based horizontal systems do not work, cannot be made to work and have never worked; they undermine teaching, distort learning as a process and do great harm**
9. **Many of our amazing teachers are stressed and exhausted. Turnover is high. Work is not the fun it was despite the smiles. There is fear. There was a better time**
10. **There has never been a time when every child and teacher has mattered less. The ECM (Every Child Matters) agenda is largely vacuous and PSHE, SEAL and Citizenship programmes are poor agents of social cohesion without VT**

It is always good to start on a cheery note, besides a teacher has to get the class's attention and teachers are not supposed to yell anymore. Many good people may find these statements over the top, confrontational and debatable but in my work with schools and my long experience as an inmate, this is what seems to be the case and I have yet to meet the non VT school that can prove these statements incorrect. The first section of this book explores this area. Unless schools recognise and understand the nature of organisational blockages it is impossible to transform to a culture of Vertical Tutoring and it is very difficult to raise standards and create a better school.

Learning as a Process

The reason why our schools are so amazing is the ability of those inside them (Heads, Teachers, Leadership Teams, Assistants) to make our schools appear to work (brilliantly in some cases) despite the obstacles put in their way. Now that may be really classy but it is also a major problem. Such exceptional people are sometimes so good at what they do that they make teaching a difficult group look easy, or running a complex school in the way they do seem possible. Similarly, Heads of Year perform miracles of time management and seem to know the names of hundreds of students and all of their intricate case histories (variation in part). SENCOs do amazing work and LSAs similarly. Form tutors with groups of 30 students are often passionate about their kids. Our schools are blessed with outstanding people and that's why it is a problem. Many realise that they are doing a job that has been made more difficult than it should be; others accept their lot as normal practice. Horizontally operated schools use very similar systems; all operate within a narrow range of operational practices and policies. It takes about ten minutes to understand how a year-based school operates and a lifetime to make it work! Except that it rarely ever does work as well as it should. Each item on the list above is interconnected and indicates a whole series of system thinking faults.

The Lot of the Teacher

Two basic influences start to gear the way schools organise learning and personnel structures. The first is the way schools perceive teaching and learning as a teacher-led activity; i.e. the classroom in its wider sense is where teaching and learning takes place. The second is the mass of central regulation, curriculum changes and the stream of quasi initiatives, agendas and reforms that determine much of what schools must do and to some extent how they should operate. Both must satisfy and undergo the weight of Ofsted inspection. Much of the latter determines the target-driven nature of the former and causes the school to seek improvement by investing in all kinds of classroom support strategies designed to improve student outcomes.

There are a number of immediate Systems Thinking concerns

1. Target driven cultures cause any moral compass to go awry and values to be ignored
2. A school has only so much capacity so energy must be focused wisely and in line with values
3. Only the Teachers seem to be regarded as *teachers*
4. The degree to which compliance and dependency has warped learning as process
5. The degree to which internal (staff) and external (families) customers are involved in learning as a process

Schools try to support and promote good teaching through mentoring, lesson observation, classroom visits by senior staff, lesson feedback, appraisal, rewards, departmental training, student feedback and a host of other ways. The focus of such support might involve classroom management, suitability, lesson preparation, pace issues, communications, student participation and more besides. All of this involves a considerable investment in time and support in an organisation where energy is at a premium. All of the methods suggested above may well help teaching and learning to some degree. But if they were really effective and schools reaped the reward for the great care they take, why do so many problems persist? Incidentally, the support most likely to be effective is regular visits by senior staff. The reason why is not

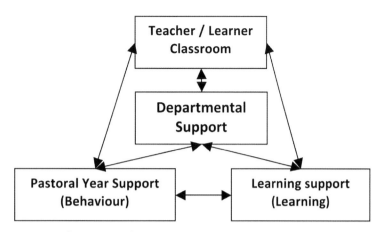

Figure 2: the Basic Classroom Support Model

what you might immediately think! It is tempting to think that the presence of senior staff is all about a show of power, making sure teachers and students are working properly. From a Systems Thinking perspective the role of managers is to act on the system not the personnel (refer back to Table 1, Ch. 1). Delightfully, instead of involving themselves in building maintenance, Health and Safety and other distractions, they are looking at learning as a process and are trying to make sure that people have what they need and that barriers to learning are removed.

The pressure on teachers is high; teachers are, after all, a profession typified by very high levels of stress. They need and deserve support. Because of this, schools seek to build other support systems to cope, many of which also come with regulations attached. The system roles are discussed in detail in later chapters.

With the basic support model in mind (fig. 2), it is worth exploring what teachers are trying to do because there may be conflict here that affects the support needed. Remember, the teacher is under intense pressure to meet attainment targets and to cover ever widening curriculum demands. Time is a big issue and is itself linked to the class being taught. Some classes need more time than others, while content coverage remains the same. Let us also take forward another thought. I have met many PSHE and RE teachers who teach over 200 students in a single day. (See Essential Schools Principles).

The *Art* of Teaching

The classroom is not what it seems. It is a whole milieu of complex learning relationships. Kids take their relationships with teachers very seriously; they're mostly very good at relationships and so are school staff; evolution has made us that way. Some learning relationships, however, take an age to form and many are damaged. Most require great teaching. And this is the point: teaching and learning is not just a technical pedagogical issue but involves a whole series of complex interactions with an extraordinary range of individuals and groups.

If we look at what teachers do, it is not easy stuff. Schools rightly demand a great deal from teachers but fail to realise that the classroom is the end part of the school's learning process and not the first part. So, what is it that makes a teacher so good that they can take risks, see learning from a student's perspective, relate learning to a child's experience and still be in full control of the class? What do teachers do? This is not a pedagogical matter alone but has more to do with the way a school is run and the psychology of learning and of groups; the first things of note when observing a really good teacher at work especially with a more challenging class seem to be simple and sophisticated all at the same time.

∞ They learn every child's first name quickly (attachment, recognition, respect)
∞ They '*read*' every child and seem to have some inner knowledge about each of them (empathy and insight)
∞ They praise more than they chide and are amazingly respectful (emotional intelligence)
∞ There is pace, a sense of achievement and fun (zest)
∞ The teacher joins in and appears to learn with them and from them (reciprocity)
∞ The students do most of the teaching and learning (activity and ownership)
∞ The room is high in emotional safety and personal value, and cherishes esteem (care)
∞ The teacher likes to work in the group and form groups (in-group loyalty formation and sense of team)

Teachers assess situations fast and are deft in their response. Similarly, kids sum up a teacher with lightning speed and know which buttons to press and how far they can push. The teacher is doing several things at once. She is using the tools and skills of her trade to build learning relationships. This has system implications for the way schools are run and learning is organised. Big ones! In particular, the observation may be made as to how exactly this relationship-building process can be achieved alongside targets, needs of challenging learners, high class numbers, time restrictions, subject coverage issues, assessment needs, liaison requirements and more besides. There is a need to know more about what we (schools) are trying to support psychologically.

Teaching and Learning: the challenge

Jonathan Haidt (2006) offers help in the form of '*the divided self*'. This may help explain the classroom situation at least in part. The mind's '*...automatic system was shaped by natural selection to trigger quick and reliable action...*' It has '*...its finger on the dopamine release button.*' Haidt describes the automatic system as '*the elephant*'. The mind's *automatic system* is fast and honed by evolution. It has been developed from the beginning and has stood the test of time. Language and reason on the other hand, are relatively recent in evolutionary terms and by the time language really took off as an evolutionary benefit, *the elephant* was already doing well on its own. Language is a much slower system that tries to reason things out and is, to use Haidt's term, '*the controlled system*'. The controlled system is '*the elephant's rider*' and is there to try and help the *elephant* make better choices, a type of '*advisor*'. This idea helps explain the classroom challenges, the controlled and automatic behavioural challenges the teacher faces and the responses she makes.

Picture a classroom full of elephants, many of which would prefer to be outside exercising more kinaesthetic learning styles and practising their multiple intelligences. They are already forming sub-groups within the classroom herd, some pro-school, some not. They are also very wary of strangers, quick to decide group make-up and are alert to any perceived threats. Some of these elephants have riders that keep their elephants roughly under control while others appear to have no riders at all. Elephants also have a herd instinct and are never quite predictable from moment to moment even though most riders get more adept at working with their elephants over time. Elephants can go crazy when the wind start to blow, hunger takes over and when conflict is in the air. Teachers know this.

When the teacher enters the room, her elephant and rider immediately pick up a huge amount of information which the teacher tries to synthesise. In fact, she has already picked up a rough picture from the noise she hears before entering the room and which tells her what to do. The teacher (rider and elephant working together) spot a riderless, mini rogue elephant hanging from the ceiling and making strange noises causing other elephants to form a mosh-pit below, unseating their riders. The teacher's elephant instantly suggests a range of immediate actions that will achieve order and produce a great dopamine reward: 1) Dive into the mosh-pit, get physical and crowd-surf 'til they wear themselves out 2) Swat the errant rogue elephant from the ceiling and crush it underfoot (technically, *give it a slap*) 3) Give a high decibel trumpet blast (*shock and awe*) to restore order. The teacher's rider takes control of the many options and chooses the best one based on the elephant's instant analysis of all the available information. The teacher (rider and elephant) stays calm, waits for the moment of maximum impact and decides another way (language and stillness) to manage the situation: *'I think we should be sitting in our seats now'*. The voice is confident, pitched to perfection and causes the child's rider to awaken (we hope) and, eventually steer his rogue elephant back to its seat, miffed at the loss of the dopamine rush.

For the teacher, it is a magical fusion of controlled (slow, reasoned) and automatic (fast, emotional and ancient) thinking synchronised by experience, confidence and expectation. Copying this is not easy, understanding it is impossible, helping others to learn from it is daunting. Indeed, learning how to do this can take forever while others can simply do it first time. Everyone's different.

What fascinates the systems thinker is fourfold

1. Teachers really are amazing people who walk towards the guns every time without flinching
2. Why is it that learning relationships start in the worst possible place: the classroom?
3. If this is the wrong place then the system support needed is very high and likely to be wrongly focused. The school learning process has been abandoned in favour of a near unworkable classroom learning process
4. Who killed the form tutor?

Asking the right question

It is so tempting to think that the teacher holds all of the class-control cards and responsibilities and to allocate blame and support accordingly. Over time, it is hoped, experience in the school of hard knocks will somehow see them through. How convenient, this *people* problem, this teacher quality problem. It seems that teaching and building the kind of learning relationships that best secure engagement with learning are inextricably linked. Is the classroom the best place and the only place to secure good learning relationships? The teacher does need support but the kind of support most needed has been removed because of the targets/values system confusion.

This is why those LTs that are on the move around the school are more likely to spot system failures and try to put them right or get help. Thankfully, many schools have at least reached that point and intuitively see vertical tutoring as a way of reuniting the school's learning process.

It is folly, therefore, to blame the teacher for any failure to engage the students in learning. It is simply unfair and wrong. The school has to function properly first.

Zoos and Circuses

The real answer rests with the tutor, the family and the re-formed mixed age peer groups. This implies that the way schools approach the business of school improvement is fundamentally flawed. The teacher is not the problem and the danger is that we make teachers the problem and see them as such. First, learning has to be a complete school process that maximises the conditions for teaching and

learning to take place. I am suggesting that schools inadvertently do the opposite. They are the hapless victims of top-down ideology of the worst kind.

VT says we can repair this link by re-engineering the system and impacting on learning as a process. We assume that we need to concentrate our organisational efforts on the classroom to make the necessary school improvement; but this is the difficult way and requires luck, experience, great insight, personality and huge energy. In all fields, some will be better than others. The Maths *course* may start in the classroom but the *learning process* doesn't, and neither do the critical learning relationships that the teacher is asked to develop in the most challenging way imaginable. Schools can employ endless techniques (video, student feedback, mentoring, shared classes, etc) for improving classroom teaching and learning, but while useful, they are only part of a process. They all depend upon getting right the important bit that is missing and without which teaching and learning is undermined: the tutor bit. Once the school's learning process is right, teaching and learning improves and develops on all fronts and classroom innovation and risk is re-enabled.

Think of a Children's Secretary in the middle of the circus ring cracking a whip and making the school elephants perform tricks and go through hoops. It is entertaining but has nothing to do with real learning and eventually everyone gets bored and switches off. Only the ringmaster fails to tire and spends his life coming up with new tricks. The real world improves not one iota and much is demeaning to sentient beings. People who work with animals are keepers; they understand how animals feel and think and what their needs are; most care in a deep sense about outcomes. Our teachers care or would if they could. School is a zoo. Blaming teachers for the shallowness of the ringmaster; that is a circus trick.

For the student, the teacher is very important for all sorts of reasons. The school exists to show how the child rider and her elephant can work together to be amazing especially when the rider practices safely and learns how. What the teacher learns and instinctively knows is how the child thinks and works and so the relationship develops. This is a *'learning relationship'*. If we understand more about learning relationships this means we can create a better supported learning process. We need a zoo that works, that cares, where keepers are humane and understand how riders and their elephants can learn together before release. Keepers understand real safeguarding; safeguarding of learning rather than the pretence of what we have now. Tutors have to be the Keepers, not (just) the teachers and this is what VT teaches. The teacher and the tutor have to work together, as one. Each is dependent on the other; both are teachers, both are customers. They are another critical learning relationship in the learning process (fig. 3 below).

From these discussions Golden Rules emerge. We should not be surprised by these *rules* because they have always been there. The problem is that the systems we have built and the erroneous strategies, reforms and regulations brought in to make them work have had dangerous side effects.

It is not sensible to create a support system whereby the only people who really understand how it operates are the students who *work* the system. Such children may talk to various teachers, a counsellor, a Connexions advisor, a Head of Year, an Inclusion Co-ordinator and more besides. But there is no one to make sense of it all for the child who roams the system and rules it. There has to be a tutor next to the child who takes responsibility for that child; who manages communications and resources. Sadly, in too many schools, it is possible for a child to go through the school without ever having a meaningful conversation with an adult.

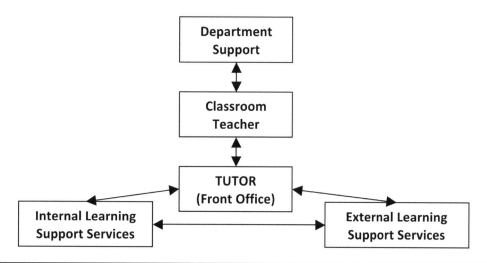

Figure 3: The Learning Process Support Model

The McKinsey Report: Assumptions Surrounding Teacher Excellence and the aspiration gene

This is a good time to look at assumptions surrounding teacher excellence and school improvement. A good starting point is the widely quoted McKinsey Report oft used by politicians across the globe as an excuse for poor policy and errant reform.

For years, this report has caused huge problems for education policy and resolved none. In fact, it has made matters worse for UK teachers and for schools because of its openness to interpretation and its failure to deal with underlying cultural and social issues. This is strange because of McKinsey's reputation as having world renowned expertise with regard to systems, processes and organisations. Here are the conclusions of its world-wide study.

1. The quality of an education system cannot exceed the quality of its teachers
2. The only way to improve outcomes is to improve instruction
3. High performance requires every child to succeed

The first conclusion is pure tautology. It seems logical, therefore to accept the second conclusion as also true. Unfortunately, it is simply not as simple as that. Governments draw spurious conclusions from such reports and so do schools. Superficially, the report suggests that it is all about the teacher, their professionalism, their desire to improve and so forth. This quickly reduces down to ideological slogans like *'every child matters'* and no *'child left behind'* and ideas about teacher excellence and the rights of children to be taught by excellent teachers. Deming would rage against such slogans as demeaning to teachers, who do not need to be told what matters. The message is that differences between cultures that *succeed* (emerging) and those that don't (mainly western) have little to do with financial investment but are simply a matter of teacher quality. This is only true in part and is open to misinterpretation.

As Schratz (2008) put it, *'Whenever I read about "best performing systems with pupils coming out on top" and manifesting "a world class education", I first think of politicians who build their wishful thinking into policy measures hoping that their fondest wishes come true.'*

According to McKinsey, a school system is entirely about the teacher in the classroom: *'You could define the entire task of a system [a school] in this way; its role is to ensure that when a teacher enters the classroom he or she has the right materials available, along with the knowledge, the capability and the ambition to take one more child up to the standard today than she did yesterday. And again tomorrow'.*

So, quite simple really: it's all about the teacher and teacher improvement. And this is what schools work on again and again (same in social work, nursing and policing) but despite their efforts progress is slow. What the Report and governments assume is that teacher quality is the problem and the challenge. But what if most teachers are already of good or high quality and that many more could be if the systems operated by schools instead of those heavily prescribed by governments, actually worked as learning processes rather than a set of highly restrictive practices and errant ideas? It is almost absurd to describe a (western) system as the classroom, especially within highly complex and classified western cultures. It is not just the teacher's capability and enthusiasm but the readiness of students to engage in learning which is critical, and this often occurs before a child arrives in the classroom and is a product of critical learning relationships developed when schools understand learning as a process, and the critical role of the personal (form) tutor. In virtually every UK school, regulations, management practices and procedures create a system that undermines the effectiveness of the teacher as the child enters the school, long before the child enters the classroom. The whole school system impacts on learning as a process; the responsibility is not the teacher's alone but that of the system that is there to enable and drive learning.

Systems thinkers (ironically, McKinsey should understand this) have something to say on this issue which helps. King and Frick (1999) describe the complex SIGGS Theory Model (set, information graphs and general systems theory) based on the school system ideas of Maccia and Maccia.

'Perhaps the simplest place to start, is (Elizabeth) Steiner's (1988) description of an "educational system." According to her work, educational systems are comprised of four components: teachers, students, content, and context. A student is defined as someone who intends to learn through guidance from a teacher; whereas a learner is someone who attempts to learn on his or her own. Content refers to what is actually learned; and context is the setting in which the content is mastered.'

In those cultures described as *world class* and *successful* is it really true that teachers (there) are any different in quality from other teachers in cultures that do not appear to perform so well (here)? Context is important and so is something that concerns governments in the west; *aspiration*. Countries with a strong cultural dynamic whereby students aspire and wish to submit to learning in order to improve (even in classes of 50 and above) allow the teacher to be effective, respected and of *high quality*. In the west, where society is fragmented and where governments aspire to be all things to all people, aspiration is diminished, and especially so at the broken bases of the culture where aspiration should be highest. Our students may choose to submit to learning in school, or to their sub-culture, their peers, their family or the gang. They have choices and may not feel the same cultural need to aspire. They will never feel *hunger* in Sizer's terms because governments try to live their life for them.

It is this that draws the lie and it is an irony that those who profess to be system leaders make such crass judgements on teachers when the system undermines them. Teachers are praised and blamed accordingly for success and failure, when all too often it is the way schools manage learning as a holistic systems process that is the real problem. Like the good Boxer in *Animal Farm,* teachers readily accept the blame and the slogan, *'I must work harder'.* There is evidence and enough common sense (Sue Palmer 1996) to suggest that schools have become part of *'Toxic Childhood'* rather than the antidote. Teachers are not to blame: this is a lie.

Tom Toms

In short, the road to world-class schools, according to my trusted satellite navigation system, is in a different direction to the one we seem to be travelling and only a handful of schools are actually going that way and are likely to get there. Unfortunately, such schools rarely hang around and quickly lose any real contact with the rest of the pack and often talk an entirely different language. Neither are they easily copied. The vast majority of our state schools are on a winding road paved with good intentions; like elephants they go from one watering hole to another and are easily led. But if they care to glance back from where they have come, they will see the path travelled littered with abandoned initiatives and the massive waste of human endeavour. Our schools try so hard to improve. So far, it has been an expensive, ideological, experimental and unsafe journey that ignores the advice of travellers, scouts and explorers and one which has seen too many falling along the way. Think of Vertical Tutoring as an extension of the scrappage scheme for old bangers: you trade in your old system and get a brand new one in return at no cost. Got to be a bargain, guv!

Some Golden Rules

1. Learning relationships are critical to learning and especially for those challenged by learning
2. Reciprocity and attachment underpin and drive many of the pre-conditions of western learning relationships and these inform us about learning as a process and how to organise schools better
3. Learning relationships between people are the basis for teaching and learning capability and successful outcomes
4. Tutors are the key to learning as a whole school process, not the teacher. The teacher and the learner depend upon the tutor as the key to learning as a process in most schools if not all schools

These are the preconditions for teaching and learning. The McKinsey Report is wrong in substance and very wrong in ignoring Systems Thinking. McKinsey is right to want to raise standards of teaching but wrong to suggest that teaching somehow stands alone and immune from other system factors.

Chapter 3: Learning Relationships and the Start of Learning as a Process

Groups, moral purpose and schools as organisation

The partnerships that should determine education as a public service have become uncertain and lopsided and have had a detrimental effect on schools and the way they are managed. Instead of a high quality system built on trust, we have created a linear model whereby the DCFS tries to perform the roles of customer and commissioner. It decides what parents want, tells schools what to do, when and how but blames teachers when things go wrong and don't do as they're told. In such a system, all innovation comes from the centre, but there is a flaw. Government is lousy at running anything of value. Public systems are built on micro partnerships not macro ones. This means that the relationship at the interface where the system and customer meet is all important; it is here where partnership is undermined by the linear model (Fig 4).

Figure 4: Partnership by Proxy

Any separation between families and schools disobeys basic Systems Thinking and weakens schools. If trust is lost between customer and supplier (family and school), the centralist tendency is to increase accountability, increase complaint litigation, increase punishment and increase inspection to weed school faults out. All of this strengthens compliance but weakens schools as organisations.

These macro relationships between government, families and schools have a negative knock-on effect all the way to the classroom and this is evident in the most important relationships of all: those learning relationships, negative and positive, formal and informal, that determine the immediate micro world of the child. The more separation there is between schools and families, the more schools are regulated, the more difficult teaching and learning becomes.

The challenge for schools is to show that they can facilitate the learning and teaching work, be places of high value and deliver positive outcomes. To achieve this, learning has to be a joined up process. Let us conveniently leave outcomes for the present as simply the result of schooling and set aside curriculum as whatever the government determines it to be. A big part of Systems Thinking is to provide an understanding of why organisations fail, why work doesn't work and how service organisations like schools can improve. In essence, we need an appreciation of why learning relationships between staff and students (all schools say these are vital) need considerably more of our *'undivided'* attention and less assumption. The first half of this book is mainly devoted to *systems checking* and the second half to systems building and establishing learning as a more effective, efficient and joyous process.

Cultural transformation to a Vertical Tutoring (VT) system stabilises and establishes schools as learning organisations and creates a safer and more effective platform for learning to take place. VT also indicates the nature and purpose of learning; but to leap to VT without understanding where we are presents VT as just another management option that can be played with and bolted-on to existing school machinery and practices: such a course of action will have no substantive value. To introduce VT without doing the system checks is to invite disaster. System checking will reveal the extent of the damage and I can let readers into a secret: most of the kit is broken, has been for ages.

In essence there is no real alternative to VT but to understand why that is so means coming to terms with a simple fact. What is happening in and to our amazing schools is wrong and it is wrong in terms of relationships, learning and the systems we are using. The curriculum is not the issue: it has been in abeyance for decades and can wait a moment longer. The priority is to get our schools running better and to re-establish a firm basis that enables learning to be more valued by the wider community than it is. Unless schools see that their moral compass is broken and their work no longer values driven but target driven, the transformation to VT cannot be achieved; across the country, these errors are causing many schools to re-invent the past while thinking they are transforming to a new culture of VT.

Changing the Nature of Debate

The Cambridge Report into Primary Education (2009) made a number of critical remarks about system practice and policy. It referred to ' *a state theory of learning*' and concerns about '*...the way the apparatus of targets, testing, performance tables, national strategies and Inspection is believed to distort children's primary schooling for questionable returns.*' This report is an excellent piece of work but picking a fight, albeit a gentle one, with government means only one winner. Further, the report is right but where to go? This excellent report, six years in the making, was rejected and summarily dismissed on day one and few had the energy to object. Beneath the many important issues raised in the report are learning relationships and it is these that can enable schools to transform themselves and approach the sanity of the Cambridge Report from another direction and without reference to the centre.

This means that schools need a different strategy to create better schools. Research and reports rarely help and most get misinterpreted and compromised and make the system worse. They do this because ideologies are selective and rely on *assertive bias* to build public systems. It was this same bias that made city bankers believe they were invulnerable and that the small voices of doubt at the periphery did not matter. In this respect, we seem to be witness to a game forever being played out in the name of education. To join in the political power game simply leads to debate and entrenched positions so it is wise to stand back (a little) and see what else can be achieved; a little lateral thinking. No matter whether government is to the centre left or right, the big system of education delivery is invariably 'conservative' in nature. It is about order, cost control, standards, value for money and structural solutions to social improvement; but the cost of such a seemingly ordered system is collateral damage at the base of the system where the most vulnerable, those 'not selected' and those whose gifts don't always fit, play out their lives. Let me put that conservatively at about 50% of young people for whom school could be a better learning experience. We can include in this number those children who '*do school, do college*' and '*do University*' and who see education as a place to collect grades to get the job that wins the game. There are more in this group than we think. Schooling should be a learning experience in the widest sense, an inner journey and not something that the more able simply *do* or where the vulnerable learn all about rejection.

The social, moral and learning world of many children is often of a different order to the school's learning world and seems to be unusually resistant to any assimilation. There is a divergence of values in our systems and in our learning relationships and this is not healthy for society or for individual citizens. The recent Cambridge Report represents the liberal argument to government to be more open and trusting and even invite a little bit more risk and chaos: it invites politicians to loosen up and take a little Prozac.

The government team found the report *'Disappointing'* and kicked it out of court! There was no debate or discussion. Both sides claim to be right in exercising their truth. To enter the debate is tempting (and actually caused me to rewrite much of this book!) but that is folly because it means falling victim to *'in-group loyalty'* and in-group loyalty cuts down *'openness to experience'* and the views of others as we shall see. Besides, why take sides when you can upset everyone? Anyway I am right. I see it clearly: both of the others are wrong. My group wins.

VT invites us to a world where this debate goes away (for a while).

Groups, Moral Psychology and the School's Learning Process

Let me begin by saying that I am singularly unqualified to offer a single word of sanity in the field of moral psychology but I shall try. The moral foundations theory of Haidt and Joseph (2007) building in part on Pinker (2002) seem to provide as good an explanation as any of how VT works at a psychological level and as an organisational process. It is suggested that there are five innate *'foundations'* which cross all cultures and which make up the moral mind.

These are

- ∞ Harm / care
- ∞ Fairness / reciprocity
- ∞ In-group loyalty
- ∞ Authority / respect
- ∞ Purity / sanctity

Teachers tend to find themselves engaged with the first two in the list above as far as (moral) behaviour is concerned. These encompass behavioural areas where the school tries to intervene and put things right, to improve behaviour and explain why. This invites the standard classroom approach (in part) way to managing and changing behaviour, some of which may be deep-seated. However, it is the notion of *in-group loyalty* that attracts attention because schools may not (have not) got this right and may again be making wrong assumptions and organising the learning / teaching process the wrong way round. Haidt (Ted.com) synthesises the following ideas (below) to explain different group behaviours and thinking between conservative and liberal.

- ∞ In-group loyalty: (psychological predisposition to be in groups and be guided by group thinking)
- ∞ Openness to experience: (personality trait affected by the groups we join)
- ∞ The development of the moral mind (schools might call this *moral purpose*)

Using Haidt's synthesis it is possible to show how all three appear to be directly connected with learning as a school Systems Thinking process. It is also possible to show how schools can better understand the interface between the school as an organisation, the direct influences on the learning behaviour of each individual, and what approaches schools should and should not adopt to intervene in order to engage a child in learning and build quality in.

In-group loyalty it is proposed, is part of the moral first draft that drives behaviour. People like being in groups, regardless of the group size, and these have a powerful shaping influence on behaviour.

However, the psychology of the team influences the way we think. It does this by shutting down our *'openness to experience'*. One trait of being human within the *'Five Factor Personality Model'* is *'openness to experience'* (McCrae 1996) and the degree to which this personality trait is expressed explains much of human behaviour. In broad terms, such *openness* to experience from a child's point of view might be seen as a willingness to learn or wanting to learn.

The more interesting manifestation here is not so much in the big system groups of education where the liberal and conservative in-group loyalty teams (DCFS v 2009 Cambridge Report) gather to debate intellectual validity and research, but in the small in-group loyalty of Team Child. The child belongs to Team School, Team Family, Team Peer Group, Team Football Fan etc all of which form the close experiential domains of 'Team Child'. These are the groups most likely to directly impact and influence learning success (openness to experience) and (moral) behaviour. By focusing on the big and powerful pressure groups that claim bragging rights over education and gain the governmental ear, we ignore the smaller world of children as learners which is something far more significant.

It is the child's small in-group loyalty that holds the real clues to running a great school where learning is a joined-up process, and it is precisely here where schools invariably go wrong.

However we decide what the output end of the school should be and however we try to answer the question about what schools are for, moral psychology provides a way forward that correlates with a Systems Thinking approach to learning: building a carefully designed process that connects the *'child groupie'* to learning. At the input end of schools, where relationships first form (birth, family, friends, schooling) learning is being shaped and children are joining groups and forming groups. People, especially young people, change their mind. Children enter the world not as *tabula rasa* but with the *'first draft'* of their moral mind already programmed-in (Marcus 2004). *'Nature provides a first draft, which experience then revises...'* Such a first draft is *'...organised in advance of experience...'* and is in a form that is *'malleable'*. Nature supplies the blueprint, and experience (nurture in part) does much of the rest.

Such a synthesis suggests that when a child first arrives at school, much is already in place especially with regard to learning and the groups a child is likely to join. The role of the school is deeply important as a formative shaper of the learning mind (co-organiser of experience) in partnership with families and friends. But the school may be in stiff competition with the rest of Team Child's loyalty groups that may have closed down openness to learning. These small and powerful loyalty groups of family and peers already have a hold on the child's engagement with learning (positive and negative) and on the first revisions of the moral mind, as attitudes to learning and to school start to form; to increase openness, the school is often on the back foot as far as successful intervention is concerned.

If this is so and common sense says that this is the case, schools need to be far cleverer in how they go about nurturing learning relationships and making them secure and especially on entry to any particular school phase. It seems logical that schools are there to ensure and prolong a young person's engagement with learning as a lifetime activity, maintaining their *openness to experience*. This is not restricted to the classroom but lies in the totality of ways in which schools facilitate and organise social in-group loyalty experiences and learning support. In other words, *'in-group loyalty'* and in-group thinking form the substantive part of a child's social environment and have a powerful shaping influence on the child's (moral) mind and on any subsequent engagement with learning in school. In essence, family and friendship groups deeply influence the degree to which a child engages with learning before the child sets foot in the school.

The need for group membership, perhaps especially in young people, prevents consideration of other valid views and places us in what Haidt calls, *'a moral maze'*. More than ever today we have children of the hive. They arrive as members of groups of different kinds, and want to be in groups and even gangs. Many seem to want to support Manchester United, Arsenal or Chelsea. Most arrive with views, attitudes and expectations about schools, careers, teachers and learning; some are positive, many negative, uncertain, anxious and vulnerable.

If this is so, the way that schools are organised to *'nurture'* and support learning requires considerably more thought than is currently the case and especially so if there is a powerful in-group predisposition for a child to learn from group membership of the class, peer groups, year group, House and family. If a child is loyal to a dynamic that derives from a group that is anti-school and anti-learning, the school as an organisation needs to rethink what it does (how it organises an effective [intervention] process) to counter and remodel this powerful innate, group predisposition. It needs to change its management assumptions about what works on day one of schooling and not leave matters to the classroom teacher to perform his/her magic. Neither can the partnership link between the family (Team Home) and Team School be assumed and taken for granted as it is now.

A Revised Partnership

What seems to be essential in building a school learning process is recognition of the influence of the child's immediate loyalty groups both in and around the school and at home, because these are most likely to affect a child's engagement with learning. The action of the school is to guide, influence, counter and support as appropriate to maximise learning by relating to the elephant's driver. The elephant just likes the safety of the herd, his family and 'mates'. When a school admits children who may, for example, come from disadvantaged backgrounds and places them into a group of their peers as schools do, the chances of intervention are slim and this impacts negatively on learning (openness to experience). Team loyalties (see research below) can have a powerful and negative influence as shapers of learning before we get to the many other organisational influences (Brighouse 2008): their psychological impact is always to *'shut down openness to experience'*. If membership of a loyalty group does act to shut down any openness to experience, any access to learning and any deeper understanding of moral values such as fairness, empathy and our endless search for what is true is likely to be restricted. Such a state of affairs cannot easily be remedied by programmes in Citizenship and SEAL and PSHE because intervention at the level of the class is not guaranteed and enjoys limited success. The school has to intervene before the child goes into the classroom and this is what VT does and is what virtually all schools fail to do.

Such loyalty groups and the child's ability to be open and able to cope with group loyalty issues in a moral and social way are at the very heart of Vertical Tutoring. It is not something we should teach as a programme but is something schools should enable and nurture in a variety of practical and learning ways. **The child has to be 'open to experience' in order to successfully engage in learning, and this means that the groups that schools form around children and the way they are formed are among the most important activities of the school and are the basis of successful teaching and learning.**

Dangerous and High Risk activities on Day One of secondary school

1. **Give the tutor the two or more hours with his/her tutor group to 'bond'**
2. **Start teaching straight away or ASAP**
3. **Let the new ones find their feet**
4. **Teach SEAL across the school**

The concept at the very heart of VT is that *relationships* come first, not teaching *'Relationships'* as a topic, but forming relationships. It is this which makes the role of the tutor pivotal to the success of learning as a process, and it is the tutor who starts the learning process by forming new micro support groups around the tutee capable of exploiting the *'malleability'* of the moral blueprint in positive ways that enable engagement with learning and a greater openness to experience.

Implications and the Power of the Pack

In many respects, teaching programmes can only be effective if there is openness to learning and while some great teachers can achieve this, not everyone can. It is the tutor who holds the key to successful engagement with learning, not just the teacher. None of the above provides a justification for a belief that mass education programmes cure social problems and counter bad influences and wrong thinking brought into school by errant loyalty group membership and powerful media influences. SEAL, Sex Education, Citizenship, PSHE and the like may enjoy limited success with those who already have in-group school loyalty to school and supportive parents, but can be counter-productive and merely assumed to be of value for many others who don't. Educationists and governments believe that teachers should teach programmes to classes to bring about desired changes (improve social cohesion) and have failed to realise that such an approach is not working as well as expected: systems are front-loaded with assumptions and so we reinvent Sex Ed. to include *'relationship education'*; schools introduce SEAL as another social cure. PSHE is made compulsory (all taught by great teachers) and we hope it works next time round and are frustrated when nothing seems to change as schools battle with forces way beyond the control and capability of most teachers (TV, Media, Video Games, Family, Peer, poor role models and loyalty to the gang) and fail to make an impact and may even make matters worse.

Learning Relationships (VT style) do not come about from teaching programmes but from a deeper in-group loyalty gene that responds directly to people. It is why the teacher in the classroom, described earlier, is so amazing; but to think she is the answer causes schools to build a learning culture in the wrong way. The brilliant teacher is the problem because we think everybody can be like her and the amazing Year Head and the Headteacher who turned the school around… if only we could find the magic formula and copy them. To make teachers and learners better starts outside of the classroom, not inside it and involves the way the school builds learning relationships and especially the way learning as a process is organised and understood. Such a process requires an understanding of the values, partnerships principles and psychology in play. Curriculum comes second until this is done.

Vertical tutoring allows the school to create its own powerful tutor-based, loyalty groups, involving parents and employing other students as leaders and mentors to create a win/win situation; these interventions keep open the door to learning experiences and are powerful enough to counter balance negative forces. All of this hinges on the ability of the school to build positive learning relationships centred on the child's Vertical Tutor. Critical to this is the positive leadership intervention of other children (mentors), a new relationship with the family and a clear understanding of the psychology within which Vertical Tutor groups operate. This is the bit that schools (all schools) so easily mess up!

Research

I am often asked about research and VT of which there is very little. Great care must be taken when doing research in schools because what schools claim as due process and what they do, especially in the way they handle variation, will influence findings. Research can only be done in those schools that are genuinely VT in their culture and learning process (conditions set out elsewhere in this book). Wherever one looks, the theory and research has already been done to some extent. In Durkheim's work on suicide, he makes the connection between belonging to different groups and being alone. Groups and belonging are essential to people and are reflected in illness and suicide rates. Steiner's 12 lectures on childhood given in Torquay in 1924 when he was a very ill man are almost spiritual in the way they describe 'the whole child', learning and the idea of nurture. Steiner Schools are hugely values driven, reverent to the way children learn and almost ignore 'time' as a constraint. Bruner's (1963) work on *'The Process of Education'* divides learning into structure, readiness, intuitive thinking and motivation. While Bruner tells us of the importance of *process* and of the teacher knowing her subject well, Sternberg (1998) reveals, in part, the folly of today's schools. We learn wisdom from adversity; it cannot be taught as such but wisdom may require the support of the group and in this case, the wisdom of the child's tutor to help *adaptation, shaping* and *selection* to overcome it. In creating a mature vertically tutored school, there is little that is new. Heads merely have to follow the footsteps of humanitarians rather than ideological fools. They will always reach the future faster and safer.

What our current model of education has done is erode and downgrade the critical role of the child's form tutor and made it into a damage limitation exercise in schools. We have a system dependent on all teachers being of the very highest ability and no country has that though we have most! We then judge the 'good' as being inadequate or poor by looking at the wrong measurement comparator and the wrong causal school improvement factors. Year group tutoring as practised in English schools today is the saddest and the most damaging and backward change ever made in schools, and there is hardly a state school anywhere that has not been coerced into prolonging this managerial mistake. The damage done to many children and their wellbeing is close to incalculable. Our inspectors are left measuring the wrong things in the wrong place in the wrong ways because in part, they are no longer values driven and too many have only a limited understanding of learning as a process. They have become the checker at the end of the conveyor belt, reporting on the paranoia of governments. Our schools too, are doing the wrong things, dangerous things. Schools have been busy creating an in-group, year-based loyalty system that is too often anti-school and anti-learning and when schools turn for support, parents aren't always there for them because we have neglected Team Family. Our schools have not kept pace with social change and new western childhood needs; except that these needs are ancient needs; 'tacit knowledge', in Sternberg's wisdom terminology. It is an irony that teachers must pass a bi-annual 'safeguarding children' course that completely ignores and bypasses the real learning dangers to children created by the system. How crazy is that?

Children arrive at school already complex. They may be badly influenced by gang culture, family life, health issues, psychological issues and more besides; all will influence what Sternberg calls their ability to balance their own needs and the needs of others. They may arrive selfish, self-centred and unaccepting of the views of others. The job of the school is to provide experiences that enable the child to 'change' in order to fit with the new environment, 'shape' to change their environment and 'select' or choose a new environment. When schools place that child in a classroom of its peers, they are relying on many teachers to resolve a whole complexity of issues without proper support and system process. Schools, horizontally run, may accidentally create and support gang culture and negative peer pressures because they are unable to create significant mixed-age, small loyalty groups around learners and learning.

VT and the critical role of the Vertical Tutor

In effect, schools organised horizontally in the way most are, allow powerful loyalty groups to form around the vulnerable, the impressionable, the ignored and the underachieving that can shut down engagement with learning and *openness to experience*. All schools seem to allow and promote this negative learning relationship 'process' while thinking they are creating a positive learning relationship process. They do this on day one when the new intake arrives when they give the tutor anything from an hour to a full day to be with their tutor group. They assume relationships will somehow form through the assumed benefits of the activities they do. They are so very wrong and the Law of Opposite Intentions quickly cuts in. Few of us are that good. Psychology is rarely practised in such a bizarre way with such a variety of people, and then only by experts.

What Vertical Tutoring does is build different in-house, mixed-age loyalty groups around the child that are high in moral values such as reciprocity, empathy, fairness, support and a redefined version of what it is to truly *care*. The key one of these is the tutor / tutee relationship which is expanded to include other tutees. VT also redefines and re-engages other loyalty groups as partners, such as Team Family. In this way VT acts on the way that the moral mind is shaped by nurturing access to new or reconstituted loyalty groups that are more *open to experience*, higher in moral understanding and which best represent the idea of a village community or extended family. New, purpose-built and tutor operated mixed-age groups keep the pathways of openness to learning clear rather than close them down; this is in preference to the idea that *social repair* programmes alone will somehow be a social cure: always, relationships before programmes, relationships before programmes.

Not only is VT a safer and more humane way of starting and underpinning a learning process but the child's tutor takes on a wider role as guide, facilitator, mentor and advocate. Relationships come first; schools say so! The tutor as healer, the tutees operating as the welcoming *pack*.

During training sessions on VT, (well over 150 individual schools and around 15000 secondary staff using horizontal Year group systems) I ask teachers and support staff to assess the influence on learning, positive and negative, of teachers, parents, tutors and peers. The question posed is this:

Who has the most influence on a child's learning, (positive and negative combined) of teachers, tutors, peers and family?

Teaching and support staff were asked to rank these in order and apply a percentage score. The answers remain remarkably consistent across all secondary schools (grammars, private, comprehensive 11-16, 11-18, single sex, C of E, RC etc) regardless of type.

Table 2: Research: Who has the most influence (good and bad combined) on a child's learning?

Choice:	Rank Order:	% age Influence on Learning
Parents	1	35-45%
Peers	2	30-40%
Teachers	3	15-20%
Tutor	4	5% or less

All of the schools surveyed were horizontally structured (Year grouped). They clearly said that tutor influence on student learning was the lowest (5% or less). Teachers, as ever, were hypercritical of themselves and placed themselves third. Parents and peers were the highest by far with parents just winning out but eventually matched by peers as peer age increased. A number of general conclusions can be drawn when these were further investigated (Barnard 2009).

1. Tutors feel undervalued, ineffective and uncertain about their role in Year systems. Highly effective tutors think the year system works. The vast majority do not.
2. The family is seen as the most important influence on learning
3. Teachers undervalue their impact and feel less effective than they are
4. Peers in horizontal systems have a very powerful influence on learning, not always positive!

This research backs the psychology of the previous chapter and is an indicator of the ineffectiveness of current learning systems in countering closed mindedness and negative learning behaviours.

When the same survey is conducted in a mature and values driven VT school, the results are very different. The tutor feels more skilled, able and professional and the values even out. There are several points to consider.

∞ If parents and peers are so important, these are the people schools need to engage with at a deeper partnership and operational level than is the case now in order to build in quality and to make teaching and learning better supported and more effective; especially so if in-group family loyalty has a negative influence on learning

∞ The status and role of the tutor has to be reinstated and revived. The tutor is the person best placed to engage with parents and students given the right system (vertical) but is least effective in a year grouped system (horizontal) and there is strong evidence to show that the tutor and tutoring in year systems has a negative impact on teaching and learning

∞ If peer groups are such an influence, we need to take great care when endorsing year organisation and especially so at the level of the tutor group. Such powerful groups are more difficult to access and turn around over time. Children can so easily be lost in such a system and not always by choice. It is a natural disposition for the children of the hive. Year systems confer and transfer power to peers creating the potential for negative learning and social imbalance in the school

∞ Finally, we can assume that if programmed intervention strategies worked, school workers would not have the perception of learning effectiveness they clearly perceive

Of course, research is problematic. Nearly all educational research in Year System schools assumes the Year System to be the norm and OK, the pastoral system to be highly effective, teaching and learning to be well supported, workforce reform to be working and tutors to be important and valued. All of these assumptions are wrong and will be seen to be system and learning process faults.

There has been almost a complete failure to realise that the current horizontal system has a global and negative influence and especially in the way it impacts on teaching and learning (the subversive mechanism for this is detailed throughout). This renders the advice given to government by think tanks and others as highly suspect. What VT does is underpin the idea that mixed age tutor groups (reproducing the essence of family) always has a positive rather than negative influence, by establishing tutees as leaders and mentors and broadening care holistically to embrace and recreate the best of family values in the school and a deeper appreciation of the 'whole child'. The effect of reviving learning relationships between tutor and tutee and family upgrades the status of all parties and forms the most consistent and powerful group (parent/tutor/student) at the critical start of the learning process. It is here that the system is made safe, where value is in-built and where learning becomes valued and supported.

If our tutors see themselves as important but impotent at the same time, as the research above suggests, such role confusion has to be addressed; especially as most tutors are also teachers. Schools need to enable the form tutor to be that magnificent person working at the very front line of the school. This is what VT does and it is this tutor role (the spirit guide, the healer, the mentor and advocate) that is the centrepiece of the cultural change to Vertical Tutoring.

The tutor's role as mentor and advocate counterbalances and re-builds the teams that form a child's immediate loyalty groups by establishing new support groups around the student in school, and a new group, the 'Front Office', comprising school and family. The challenge is to establish a positive and powerful vertical structure that is stable and lasting, thus moving the school as an organisation from 'assumed' relationships to something deep, safe, substantive and engaging. This keeps the channel of *'openness to experience'* clear, maximising and enriching the moral and learning experiences acting upon Nature's *'first moral draft'* : the humble tutor as a conduit, healer and spirit guide, the lynch-pin of teaching and learning.

This concept underpins the rest of this book and is the most difficult part of it, explaining as it does *why every child does not matter* (UK) and why *so many children do get 'left behind'* (USA).

If there is a fourth Golden Rule it is hidden here:

In the 'divided self', teaching programmes as cures to impact on behaviour come from our conscious and teacher reasoning and control side; kids are mainly switched on to their 'affective' and automatic side and the call of group chemistry. It is this fissile and complementary mix of Control v. Automatic that ensures that big stratified and regulated systems are doomed to backfire in spectacular ways and require the kind of constant repair by politicians that makes things totter and get worse. What makes big systems work is not the same stuff that makes smaller human systems work. It is a failure to appreciate and celebrate the small mechanics of chaos as opposed to systems of control and targets. Just as modern psychology railed against tabula rasa, so the father of Systems Thinking, Ludwig von Bertalanffy (1968), railed against *'closed'* human systems. Life is not about the maintenance of equilibrium but the maintenance of disequilibria: people are *'active personality systems'*. The way the school engages with such personality systems complete with their inherent propensities and innate variation, requires high flexibility and relationships that are close-up and personal. You can control chaos in a classroom but the natural order is to create chaos and the great lessons contain elements of both. Working with chaos is the key but to do this requires other active personalities (tutor, parents and tutees) close by: atoms don't work by themselves and, like atoms children are a law unto themselves in their complexity. Schools have to master quantum mechanics and understand the Copenhagen Interpretation! This means thinking small...

Unless, of course, there has been some sort of behavioural change over the past 100,000 years or so but then nobody tells you anything in school nowadays. Communications in schools is always such a problem.

Jon Luc Picard fears cybernetic organisms like the Borg who are high on in-group loyalty, command and control and who forcefully insist upon team membership and total compliance. He prefers his own volunteer crew and tends to avoid the Delta Quadrant where the Borg hangs out. School tutors often see tutor time as their Delta Quadrant and do much to avoid being shanghaied as a tutor. Most school leaders and managers see the idea of no longer having a tutor group as a sure sign that they have *arrived* and become *management*; in fact, they have just left. So what is the Golden Rule?

Searching for Clues in Schools

We don't have to look far to find endless examples of learning relationships at work in schools but these weaken as students grow older. There have been many schools, mainly non-secondary, that recognise the way kids operate and learn, and build significant mixed-age support groups around the child. They do this in part by recognising the child's *first moral draft* and the way *in-group loyalty* works: they use these to nurture the development and joy of learning and of mind. They don't say that, but this is what the schools below seem to do. It is instinctive and innate, wired in from their own moral blueprint.

In Italy, Loris Malaguzzi recommended with a positive rather than a deficit model of young children (six and under). The child is seen as *'rich in potential, strong, powerful and competent'*. Importantly, he also sees the child *'connected to adults and other children'*. Learning derives from a matrix of talking, listening and interacting with adults (learning relationships and the tutorial approach used in VT). In some ways, the teacher is a learner and the child is a teacher. Learning involves constant innovation and experimentation. Schools are there to ensure children feel secure and part of a bigger family (vertical tutor in-group loyalty). There is a real and growing partnership between home, school and family, again the essence of VT and an extension of the loyalty group. Openness to experience is all. Nurturing is vital. When interviewed by Rankin (2004), Malaguzzi said that the *'indispensable'* point of working with small groups of children is to develop a personal relationship with each child that values every child. His 'Reggio' schools approach was all about collaboration and co-construction aimed at producing world citizens.

The Netherlands has a wide variety of schools from which parents are able to choose. Schools tend to be independently run and state funded including Steiner, Montessori and Jenaplan schools. (The learning philosophy of Steiner is very akin to Sternberg's idea of 'tacit' wisdom.) Again, parent participation and partnership is high and increasing as is the autonomy of schools. Compare this to our system of dependency and parental alienation across all schools. It seems that where parental involvement is high, state interference is less. English schools should note this with care. Jenaplan Schools see each student as a unique individual. The key strategy is to ensure that a child feels 'at home'. Mixed age (vertical) groupings are seen as essential. Again, parent partnership is vital to make this work. In the most innovative and child friendly schools, parents and teachers are valued participants and the curriculum increasingly personalised.

In the USA, Joyce Epstein (1995) has developed *'National Standards'* for parental involvement. (Vertical Tutoring has an even better variation on this theme, but the principles are the same.)

The Six standards

- ∞ **Communicating**: effective communications between home and school
- ∞ **Parenting**: parenting skills promoted and supported
- ∞ **Student learning**: parents involved in the child's learning
- ∞ **Volunteering**: parental involvement in school encouraged and facilitated
- ∞ **School decision-making**: parent participation
- ∞ **Collaboration with community**: community used as a resource to strengthen schools, families and learning

Schools should remember that the family needs school as much as the school needs family and to deny this can only further fragment the lives of the vulnerable, and dilute learning outcomes. Both are engaged in teaching and learning and schools need to recognise how they can support this as a partnership and process concept. Both are high on in-group loyalty. Success here leads to innovation and experimentation to see what works, and this invariably leads to greater teacher autonomy. Such schools constantly develop learning operations and processes around the 'whole child'. Should a rift between home and school emerge in an English state secondary school, the child can walk straight down the middle to another less desirable group or side with whichever (home or school) suits; either way, great damage to learning can result especially when the child becomes lost in the school's *back office* coping and repair system.

The Nature of Transformation

Epstein's descriptors are what our own secondary schools claim in the name of *partnership*: there are even top-down regulations that allude to such partnership but it does not really happen at secondary level in any substantive way and any claims otherwise are bogus. There are a few secondary schools that really do understand a process way to building parent partnership, but only a very few. Not only is parent partnership not the case but the erroneous assumption by schools that it somehow exists within their school's learning process, reflects leadership and managerial delusion, de-skilling and a tick box approach to the school as an organisation. Schools have lost touch with values and any substantive theory of learning as a process. Here, rationality and leadership appears to have been twisted by hype and spin and this is a direct reflection of an unstable partnership with the centre which distances schools from parents as the key partner customers of schools. The good intention to encourage or make the key players work together is full of assumption, and assumption always causes the law of opposite intentions to switch on.

In all of these schools and in many others lie the clues that give purpose to our need for real school transformation and to recognise that the current UK and USA system is organisationally the wrong way round as far as learning as process is concerned. The schools above share a commonality about how kids learn best: this theory embraces parents, other children (mixed age) and depends upon building and sustaining loyalty to learning relationships. All schools have to do is put the right people together in the right way in the right place and to invite them to listen carefully and encourage them to be innovative. This is school process management and this requires minimal prescription from the centre. In effect, what schools face in England and the USA, is a transformational challenge. This is all about recombining basic management understanding in a way that better lines up with the learning values and partnerships in which all schools claim to believe. Learning systems really should be simple not hypercomplex. We either make big schools into small schools by reorganising them vertically (school as four Houses with small tutor groups) or we create loads of different schools everywhere to pick and mix from. Or, we do both.

Magic

For this book, transformation is the management of cultural change to Vertical Tutoring. This is the only cost free system likely to get schools back on track and build on a more substantive theory of learning supported within learning relationships, as opposed to a state theory of targets and social repair programmes which is going nowhere and damaging many.

But there are other clues closer to home. We are always brilliant at inventing things in the UK. What we then do is throw our ideas away and let others take the credit and sell them on. As ever, among the discarded waste of the past is everything we need for the future. It is the House System, the tutor (Mr. Chips) and magical schools like 'Hogwarts'. Hidden in 'Harry Potter and the Sorcerer's Stone', Joanne Kathleen Rowling, herself a teacher of French and English, touched on one of the most important and significant moments in the learning life of a child.

'Welcome to Hogwarts,' said Professor McGonagall. 'The start-of-term banquet will begin shortly, but before you take your seats in the Great Hall, you will be sorted into your houses. The Sorting is a very important ceremony because, while you are here, your house will be something like your family within Hogwarts.'

At Hogwarts, there are four Houses; Gryffindor, Hufflepuff, Ravenclaw and Slytherin; schools within schools, groups within groups, the tutor as the wizard who makes things happen. What is of importance is the fearful ceremony as the child leaves one family (home) to temporarily join another (school). The transfer process, UK style, is fraught with difficulty and built on the erroneous assumption that tutoring occurs, despite schools having 'killed the tutor'. There is not a school I have worked with that thinks anything other than their transfer system works well and is carefully and expertly carried out. **On closer examination, every single school has built a transfer process that is hopelessly inadequate and wrong**

and dangerously so. This is not the fault of schools but of system builders. Every school apes every other school and I have not seen one that builds learning relationships or sees the shallowness and inadequacy and harm of what their systems do to tutors and students.

Later I will show how Vertical Tutoring approaches this very differently by building Front Office in-group loyalty. Transfer has to be magical because the tutor needs to be magical. Magic requires that formulas work; you have to get it right. Western schools have got their processes all wrong.

Hogwarts has much in common with our schools: there is a constant battle against the endless decrees from the Ministry of Magic. No change there, then!

Change Titles and Dance

A feature of today's schools is the way management titles have supposedly changed to fit in and comply to new system requirements. Unfortunately this largely superficial practice is not transformational, does not improve schools and adds nothing to teaching and learning. It is simple acquiescence and a perverse form of management (non-management) which adds further complexity. I have met countless teachers with the most amazing titles and job profiles. I have met many a 'Head of Every Child Matters' and numerous 'Leaders of Learning'. Recently, a Headteacher proudly told me why Heads of Year in her school are now called 'Leaders of Learning'. It is a not untypical slant on a school's response to managing variation (data and information) but without actually managing variation (hence the perversion).

'We have cracked the academic / pastoral divide. Heads of Year are no longer just pastoral people', she said, proudly. *'They are now Leaders of Learning and must look at the data of every child alongside their pastoral responsibilities, to underpin learning and monitor progress.'*

The Leadership Team all nodded in solid agreement that this was a good strategic move and sensible leadership and management. However, the Heads of Year (now *Leaders of Learning*) said that their job had not really changed at all. They were still doing pretty much the same things they had always done in the same time and on the same pay. The need to manage variation (handling data and information) is identified as important but the managerial application is simply not achievable by Heads of Year and this inevitably results in an opposite effect in terms of learning and the learning relationships. How can we have a solitary, amazing person (HOY) responsible for 200+ students, their care, their progress, their behaviour and school/home liaison? What happens when this person eventually collapses with exhaustion? And what exactly is the role of the child's tutor and the parents in all of this? Instead of transforming management and seeing learning as a human process, schools make matters worse not better by introducing delays and single channel communications blockages within an already busy and expanding back office of admin and bureaucracy.

The high ability Head of Year in a school is actually a *'super secretary'* and leads a life raging between frustration and occasional elation. In effect, the Head of Year is doing the job of her tutor team; the tutors in turn cannot do their own job because that job has been changed to petty administration and registration and their role inadvertently undermined by the school's Leadership Team. By adding to the Heads of Year responsibilities, matters have been made considerably worse not better from every perspective as old practices are concreted in. Schools treat change superficially in part because of its top down nature. The business of being a Head of Year is back office.

Schools as Back Office Systems

The reception desk of a hotel is the *'front office'* of a simple organisation. When you first contact a hotel, you get instant access to the information you need. Further information and services are available from your room but the front office remains the key point of contact. The customer is usually able to easily access the services needed so that their customer demands are met. The comfort of the room, the facilities available and the style with which services are delivered are some of the areas where quality (the capacity of the hotel to meet customer demand) is built in. Customer needs are fairly small (smoking / non-smoking, vegetarian / non vegetarian and so on) and most requirements can be 'drawn down' as needed. The customer deals almost entirely with the front office (reception) and has minimal contact, if any, with the back office (kitchens, cleaners and maintenance staff). The importance of the front office to the customer is critical. It makes life easier for busy people and is the point of access to other services. The purpose of the front office is to delight customers and make them feel valued. Another purpose of the front office is to minimise complaints (very expensive and wasteful) and maximise customer return figures. All who work in a hotel know how things work and the standards needed. Customer satisfaction is all.

There is no point in comparing a school with a hotel (unless, of course, you are Head of a brand new Academy!) but the concept of front and back offices is important when running a service organisation like a school.

Schools are hypercomplex, very busy and have to respond to high customer demand and variation. Like hotels, they have their reception office. The call system enables you to leave a message if your demand is simple (pupil absence, staff absence etc). However, when the service needed is more complex you eventually end up leaving messages in the 'back office' where all the busy people are (teachers, support staff, pastoral teams). Anything that reaches the back office enters a world of high bureaucracy, regulation, policy implementation and complex communications all run by busy people who are also trying to teach. To ease the strain, the school employs extra, equally talented people (Non Teaching Staff or Learning Support Staff) to prop up the system already stretched and under considerable time and work pressure. The back office gets bigger and even more bureaucratic so the school employs more management staff and extends the job descriptions of the LT. This is called 'Workforce Reform' except that there is no such 'reform'. Paperwork increases, computer systems have to be updated, staff offices have to be added, communications increase, stress increases, meeting frequency increases and complaints go up not down as the back office 'system' inevitably slows down. In an attempt to join systems up, the law of opposite intentions comes into play.

What the current system does is spark uncoordinated, multi-nodal responses that give the appearance of direction and purpose while managing to keep all school operatives extremely busy doing the wrong jobs in the wrong way by (in the case of back offices) the wrong people (Fig 5 below).

In the above schematic (fig. 5) there are at least 100 times more arrows (lines of communication) than indicated. The parent demand (inquiry, clarification, complaint, concern) starts at reception where parents are now offered automated choices. When they eventually do get through to a human being at reception, the person they need to speak to is unlikely to be available or may not be known by the parent who may then ask to speak to the Head who will definitely be unavailable. If the concern involves other children, there is likely to be massive internal disruption to learning and any consequent investigations may take very busy people several days to complete. If an outside agency like social services is concerned, the delays could be even longer because services are not easily 'joined up'. Communications follow any available conduits and will be constantly referred upwards and along before any resolution occurs. Thus a HOY (Head of Year) may need to see the SENCO and the Looked After Children Co-ordinator and many more besides; a Learning Support person and even the child's tutor may have information. Meanwhile, customers are waiting.

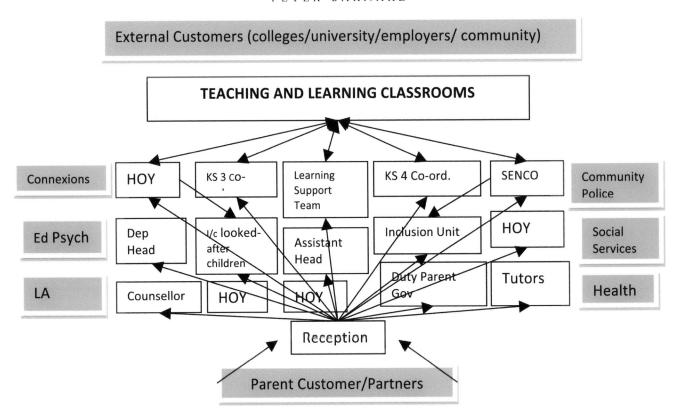

Figure 5: Creating back office blockages

Once in this system, things are delayed, deferred and lost. Neither can the system be tidied up by creating larger units, more managers and increased student support people. These simply add complications and create more hierarchies and extended bureaucracies. The French try to resolve issues with 'Monitors' and the USA with 'School Counsellors' but the English have always had the best system, 'Tutors'; but this has been all but abandoned and undermined. Not even the Ministry of Magic would do that. Top down system building and crisis management is now endemic to the way western systems operate.

Let's Play, 'Guess Where the Front Office is'

Schools have no front offices, at least not anymore. Reception is not a front office in a school. I lied about the hotel. In the hotel there are many front offices: the leisure centre has one, the restaurant, the hairdresser. The school front office has been absorbed into the back office of schools and the work redistributed; but for the most part schools destroyed them when they killed the tutor. The advent of targets as organisational levers and improvers has been matched by a loss of values. Put this together with inadequate leadership weak management training, an overdose of prescription from an ideological Children's Secretary obsessed with fairness and back offices proliferate in no time at all; the rest is history or should be.

Schools think that 'reception' is the front office but this is simply a link to the back office. The receptionist usually has some basic information but is really a conduit to other people and a filter that prevents the crazy people selling spare carpet from Heathrow Airport from getting to the Head.

The front offices in public service systems are where people go to access what they most need. These offices have not gone missing; schools have simply abandoned them and reduced their activity to an exercise in damage limitation. The problem in schools run horizontally is that the front office never ever worked as it should and all attempts to make it work have met with high failure. Only in a Vertical System can front offices do the job they were meant to do.

The Front Office, quite simply, is where the tutor works with parents and a tutee. Whenever and wherever this meeting occurs, this is the Front Office and schools should have loads of them. These are the places where Vertical Tutoring begins and learning as process starts. This is safeguarding and care in a real sense rather than the narrow regulated nonsense now prevalent in our schools. It is this that makes it possible for 'every child to matter': this and this alone.

Chapter 6: The Search for Organisational Purpose

The Purpose of the Process

If schools should be about anything, then 'one world citizenship' seems as good an aim as any. So the solution is to devise a programme to suit and order teachers to teach it. But when we put C21st kids into C20th schools, things don't quite work out the way system acolytes say they will. Peter Druker (1994) called for '...*lifelong learners who can think critically, solve problems and work collaboratively*'. Our lame programme response is to make group-work compulsory in the National Curriculum (programmes before learning relationships). To get what King (1999) calls, '*manipulators, synthesisers and creators of knowledge*', we offer children a return to thematic approaches. Nothing can make our angst about the future go away but neither should we think that there is some magic educational way of making the leap. Perhaps we would do better to get out of the way of learners rather than prescribe every move. Prozac and chaos! Whatever we do, it starts with the way we treat each other.

Futurologists who see education as being far too important for current school models, look to Systems Thinking and system design for answers and often have a starting point that embraces parents and then the community before going global. Complex organisations like schools sit between two questions: What sort of world do we need to build? What learning, support and experiences do our kids need in order to help build and be part of that world? The link between the two is learning; the teacher is the guide, the tutor the facilitator, the peer group is the local support, the parent is both and the community is the beneficiary and cheerleader. All are teachers and learners. Perhaps we should start with a simpler idea and have faith: let's get everyone keen on learning with the skills to learn. Our children will sort out the global bit; they already are.

What VT can do is create an organisation where learning can be superbly supported and give schools the management confidence to make curriculum leaps. VT seems to provide a way of un-sticking schools.

The Deeps and the Gateways

What is encouraging is the whole notion of a more bespoke approach to learning. At National Conferences, Heads identified nine 'Gateways' that seem to take things forward: however, there are 'deep' inherent traps here and great care is needed in interpretation. These 'learning gateways' to a more personalised approach to learning have been assigned by Hargreaves to the 'Deeps' as follows

Table 3: The Deeps (Hargreaves 2006)

Deep Learning	Deep Experience	Deep Leadership	Deep Support
Assessment for Learning	New Technologies	Design and Organisation	Mentoring and Teaching
Student Voice Learning to Learn	Curriculum	Workforce Reform	Advice and Guidance

Thus 'deep learning' is *'secured through personalisation'*; this is good but is far more complex than the 'Deeps' suggest. *'Deep experience'* is secured when schooling is structured so that all are *'fully engaged in their learning'*; this is the important area and the one that is exponentially challenging to schools. *'Deep support'* demands that schools *'collaborate with other institutions'* and agencies. Of course this takes time and creates bureaucracies which impact on and detract from the management of the learning process. *'Deep leadership'* is rather like Deming's 14th principle (later chapter). This involves redesigning education *'…so that through a culture of personalisation and co-construction with shared leadership, the school secures deep experience, deep support and deep learning for all its students.'* Co-construction is the involvement of students in their own learning as part of a learning and design strategy. As a group, these are not achievable as a working process in horizontal tutorial systems of management but they are precisely what Vertical Tutoring does by creating a learning process. In fact, the 'deeps' are 'shallows' as things stand. Workforce reform is a myth that has actually caused schools to stay the same and embed poor management practices. It is actually a coping mechanism for increased regulation that has caused bureaucratic back office growth. Reforms are often illusions.

According to Hargreaves, the most challenging of the nine *'gateways'* to personalised learning is School Design and Organisation. This should be no surprise. The challenge is elegantly put by King and Frick (1999)

'Just understanding this need for redesign, however, does not provide us with the necessary skills to successfully create alternative schools. All too often, reform efforts fail because we lack the abilities required for systemic design; we cannot analyse the existing school model holistically and recreate it from the ground up. Instead, we often remain entrenched in our current notions of education and only tinker at the edges of schools, making minimal changes. With the grandest of ideals, designers often aim towards creating a new school that looks totally different from traditional education, only to find that the resulting system is very similar to a traditional classroom!'

The problem seems to be that we are once again looking at programmes before relationships and this is why schools always eventually end up reinventing the factory system. It is relationships that need to be 'redesigned' first and an understanding of what conditions people need to work effectively and with joy. It is these that have implications for school design. The UK's leading systems analyst and thinker, John Seddon (2008), provides a cutting and much needed Systems Thinking analysis of failure in public services.

"We invest in the wrong things believing them to be the right things. We think inspection drives improvement, we believe people can be motivated with incentives, we think leaders need visions, managers need targets, and IT is a driver of change. These are all wrong ideas. But they have been the foundation of public 'reform'."

He describes these *'plausible'* but *'essentially wrong'* ideas as being *'promulgated through a massive specifications and inspections industry.'* Now this may sound familiar to schools! Redesign does not seem to be the totality of the learning challenge although great architecture is inspirational and uplifting. A school is a school is a school. The real challenge to schools is the way learning is managed and supported. When this is healed and re-engineered, we can think about design. We need an escape route, and to remember that public services are all about enabling people to access what they need and to make the processes used for drawing down resources as easy as possible.

Understanding Old Culture, Dead Ends and Escape Tunnels

It is helpful to draw some of the edges of the box in which 'education' and our schools are stuck based on the observations of Ted Sizer (1992).

1. Despite the different names we give to secondary schools, the student experience is remarkably similar across all of them. There is a great deal of sitting and listening, high teacher dependency and a high need for student compliance and docility. In the end, secondary schools are all about taking subjects and have been for the sum of my career. (Please note, I am aware of the fantastic extra-curricular opportunities many schools offer and the amazing achievements of schools: I simply want to establish some basics.) Vertical tutoring doesn't change this but provides a better coping support structure which enables the possibility of curriculum change and an improved classroom experience. Change starts with a better process, not a grand vision.

2. For teachers, life is equally challenging. They are compelled to see teaching and learning largely through the lens of their subject. Their immediate problem is covering increasing content and change demands and fighting for the time to do it. There are times when field trips, college links, language exchanges and exams collide causing huge staff stress. Staff tend to teach too many students and are forced to constantly reduce depth to cover breadth while managing the slog of marking and preparation. Add to this a National Curriculum with all of its strictures and the freedom to plan and innovate around learning becomes more difficult. The totality of demands is too high and is driven on by awarding points for passes. When children fall short or fail, teachers are always there to take responsibility feeling that the fault is theirs.

3. Finally, there are our amazing students. The ones from supportive families who know the school system well will usually 'do school' and 'pass subjects' and get to college with no problem. Others not so. Some suffer from an inability to read and write and do sums. They want to be entertained before boredom sets in. In the UK, we have built a whole guilt catalogue of victimology around such children. For them the system rarely works well. Schools cope by lowering expectation, separating them out and often assuming the worst (and sometimes getting it). But this makes no sense. There is always that teacher who says, '*She works well for me*' and, '*He's terrific in Drama*'. Ask the same child to run an errand, help look after a younger soul and everything changes. Children are more capable than we allow. Teachers see this but are unable to reach out and help.

It seems that all parties are impotent to break free from the routine of the factory. Ted Sizer (1992) explored the plight of the American High School in *'Horace's Compromise'*, a masterly contribution to the school improvement debate. *'One purpose for schools – education of the intellect –is obvious. The other – an education in character –is inescapable.'* But how? The answer for Sizer is to reduce the State's role to Numeracy, Literacy and Civic Understanding but this raises the whole problem of trust and this is a major partnership issue in the US and the UK. So the circularity rolls on. Hidden in *'Horace's Compromise'* are many side references to VT, the whole child and the personal tutor. It is the tutor who gives straight answers, support and the time to listen.

Sizer's own escape route was to refocus the school. He established **'The Coalition of Essential Schools'** which is also moving towards a three way deep conversation between the school, parents and the student, one of the key requisites of VT.

The principles of the *Coalition* enjoy increasing support and are set out below.

Principles:

1. The school's focus is to help students learn to use their minds well. The schools should not attempt to be "comprehensive."
2. The school's goals shall be simple: that each student should master a limited number of essential skills and areas of knowledge…. "Less Is more" should dominate.
3. The school's goals should apply to all students.
4. Teaching and learning should be personalized to the maximum feasible extent … no teacher (should) have direct responsibility for more than 80 students … decisions (about) the use of students' and teachers' time and the choice of teaching materials … must be unreservedly placed in the hands of the principal and staff.
5. The governing practical metaphor of the school should be student-as-worker.
6. The diploma shall be awarded upon a successful demonstration of mastery–an "Exhibition" … that may be jointly administered by the faculty and higher authorities…. As the diploma is awarded when earned, the school's program proceeds with no age grading.
7. The tone of the school should explicitly and self-consciously stress values of unanxious expectation … of trust … and of decency … Parents should be treated as essential collaborators.
8. The principal and teachers should perceive themselves as generalists first and specialists second.
9. Ultimate administrative and budget targets should include … substantial time for collective planning by teachers, competitive salaries for staff and an ultimate per pupil cost … not [to] exceed those at traditional schools by more than ten percent.
10. The school should demonstrate … inclusive policies (and) model democratic practices … explicitly challenging all forms of inequity and discrimination"

(Coalition of Essential Schools: *The Ten Common Principles,* (1998). Source: Wikipedia

The Principles of the US Coalition of Essential Schools (CES) are important because they unite learning as a process with the development of the moral mind within a values driven school. In simple terms, these principles are intended to secure the engagement of students with learning at a deeper level, and to map out the kind of organisational process needed to achieve such outcomes. It is not about *'coverage'* of an *'entitlement'* but more about growing good, decent citizens capable of teaching themselves (being learners as opposed to students). Students still have to show 'mastery' and personal achievement is part of the buy-in. In English schools the curriculum has become alarmingly complex in an attempt to engage all: for the CES, *'less is more'.* There is a recognition that teachers have to work with the 'whole child', the importance of 'one-to-one relationships' and the vital role that parents should play. Those schools that practise a culture of VT are already there and best placed for the next phase of the curriculum. Relationships first!

Directly there is a move away from subjects, the whole area of assessment and / for learning changes irrevocably. It becomes impossible to separate outcomes from the totality of the student. In such a CSE model, the curriculum helps *shape* the student as a person. This role has become uncertain in English schools because variation (environmental and performance information about a child) has become 'quantum' in nature (Zohars below) and schools have not been able to adapt to this. By this I mean that we cherish targets at the expenses of nurturing learning; we are too focused on the bits of the student that achieve subject targets because this is how schools and students are largely measured and, indeed, punished for any failure. We have ignored the whole child (the full variation) and our school system reflects this organisational fault in customer care and customer partnership.

Quality and the crux of the matter

It seems to me that there is a constant difficulty concerning any education debate that even our systems thinkers don't always recognise in full. Langford and Cleary (1995) (just as this book does) appeal to the 14 system management points set out by Deming (discussed later). What they say invites us to reconsider what we mean by quality and 'adding value'.

'One of the difficulties in talking about quality is its complex set of interrelationships. It is not merely tools and processes. It is not outcomes. It is not portfolio assessments. It is not even continuous improvement. And attempts to produce quality by imitating any of these or countless other strategies are doomed to failure.' This is the danger of accepting the 'Deeps' as a coherent solution.

This has a particular reference to schools trying to imitate other schools and the whole business of sharing best practice. Copying best practice rarely works well and is just as likely to damage as improve. So what is quality? According to Langford and Cleary, '...*quality is a new way of seeing and thinking about the very relationship between teacher and learner. That relationship, we believe, is framed in a fundamental context that includes understandings, practices and beliefs that enhance it and make learning happen'.* They call this *'quality learning'* and see this as integral to the principles set out by W. Edwards Deming.

For me, this helpful approach misses out on one critical step. To create the quality relationship between teacher and pupil, there has to be a quality prior relationship between the tutor and the tutee. Get this wrong and the quality teacher relationship is damaged before it has a real chance to form. In effect, only if we swap 'teacher' with 'tutor' is the definition spot on! This is the key process that schools going vertical have to understand and enable.

Otherwise, there is a major problem. Quality learning relationships cannot be achieved within the structure of schools that we have. The *repair model* of the 'counsellor' (USA), the 'Head of Year' (UK) and 'le moniteur' (France) are the main obstacles to learning while purporting to be the key facilitators and back-up system. We wrongly believe that the teacher is the single source of quality learning and quality relationships; if only we can source the magic ingredients that some teachers possess. Unfortunately, the systems that are in play today are systems tacked on to pre-existing systems that broke down an age ago because they could not cope with social change and variation, and we see this with year based pastoral care.

By a constant emphasis on establishing learning relationship, quality can be built into a school system and especially one rooted in Systems Thinking. **In short, quality relationships need to exist in classrooms and alongside classrooms for learning to succeed, but they actually begin with the teacher as tutor outside of the classroom and with very small groups and with the involvement of parents and student mentors.**

We should compare the ten Essential Schools Principles with what we do in the UK. The Essential Schools Principles lead us back to the moral mind and to Haidt and Joseph's expanded *'First Draft'*. Harm / care; Fairness / reciprocity; In-group loyalty; Authority / respect and Purity / sanctity.

Values driven schools, as opposed to target driven schools (what we have), have to combine an understanding of morality with a clear idea of how relationships best develop for learning to take place.

This in turn requires a school to develop a learning process that is based on sound management principles that can work in harmony with what it is to be human and humane (joy of work). If there is failure in our schools it might well relate to the degree to which schools recognise such moral foundations, and understand their relationship to the school as an organisation and the way the school operates. Such a concept has to be made operational and workable long before we start blaming teachers when things go wrong. To get our schools working well requires an understanding of how we best support learning relationships prior to classroom relationships, although the two are inextricably connected.

If such innate intuitions influence the moral draft that children arrive with, they also provide the dimensions within which the child starts to perceive and make sense of the world. Schools need to recognise them and nurture safe development. Inherent here are the insecure values that children appeal to again and again. *'It isn't fair: you don't care: I didn't mean to: I'm not grassing on my mates: you don't respect me, why should I respect you? Who do you think you are? She called me names: it's his fault: why should I care? You don't understand: it's boring: it's not my job: he started it'.* Sound familiar?

And then we come to the family in-group loyalty: *'my child never lies: I know my child: my child said it was the other child's fault: my child has a personality clash with the teacher.'* All are difficult to resolve and counter unless the school has established trust and agreement that teaching and the management of variation requires partnership. Vertical tutoring should ensure that the relationship between home and school should not be more than a cigarette paper in width and that there should be no gap at all between tutor and tutee.

Just where in the school should these relationships best be nurtured and how? The negative answer is NOT THROUGH TEACHING PROGRAMMES, at least not until learning relationships have been formed and the school really takes the high value aims and objectives it sets itself more seriously than is the case. Programmes are not cure-alls for all. They supplement and complement and eventually enable. This will become very clear when we go deeper into the school and the front office. It starts with family, then with the tutor in the Front Office, then the immediate vertical tutor group and then teaching programmes. Eventually, Headteachers may come to see that when tutor/tutee relationships start to work and older students see themselves as leaders, learning opens up. RELATIONSHIPS FIRST: this is because these impact on in-group loyalty and offer the better chance of allowing the moral mind to develop safely and strongly. In this way VT not only builds the first part of learning as a process, but it continues to work on the moral mind, citizenship and community so underpinning the work of the teacher. Without the vertical tutor, the tutee as leader and mentor and the parent as teacher, there can be no coherent learning process.

Values and Systems Thinking go together. Great Headteachers and Mavericks know that what you do is build quality in from the beginning and keep building it in: moral quality, values driven.

In this context, the best education and learning is not the single domain of the classroom. Those who think it is are likely to face much disappointment and should not be running schools. As Ted Sizer said (1984), *'Students learn much from the way a school is run'*, a quote rightly used by Hargreaves (2006). Vertical Tutoring says that students learn virtually everything of importance from the way a school is run.

If this moral blueprint is truly cross cultural, we have the moral purpose of schools; global citizenship. This doesn't mean implementing programmes and world studies in infant schools. Schools need to facilitate: our kids, together with their personal tutor/life coach, are more than capable of doing the rest: forming big groups is built-in for the children of the hive, but it starts with the tutor and the parent and

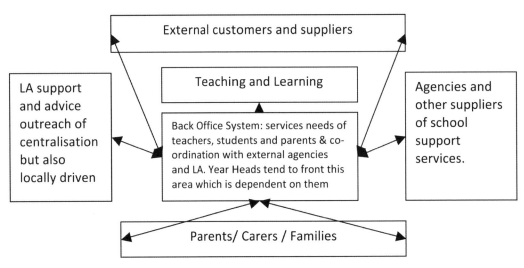

Figure 6: The Basic Year System Model (Back Office)

the child in every school including secondary schools. The first stage is obvious from both an educational and a Systems Thinking point of view. We need to recreate the idea of family within our schools and work with families alongside the school. **Front offices nestling in Vertical Tutor Groups (mini–schools) nestling within House schools nestling within the big school, nestling in the community, nestling in a global community all in touch and all trying to build something better than what we have: this is vertical tutoring and the first step.**

All over the world including the UK, there are schools striving for a values driven approach to learning rather than a command system. Most schools have drifted into the back office model (fig.6) and set out here in its generalised form.

In this model there are other critical customer side effects. By removing the tutor as the link with families, not only have we put schools under severe organisational pressure but we have put families under pressure by devaluing their already fragile role and making them dependent on schools. Such a system of dependency; pupils on teachers, families on schools, schools on the DCSF can go nowhere worthwhile except round in circles. We have effectively extended the dependency culture right down the line to the child who is spoon-fed teaching to the target. There are further knock on consequences when the school is made into a back office organisation.

∞ Teaching and learning will never be properly supported and this gives the erroneous impression that teaching is at fault
∞ Vulnerable students will quickly find or be victims of any weak points in a complex system and can easily exploit or reject the system accordingly. In effect, this allows the 'recalcitrant' students to be the only people able to innovatively 'work' the system!
∞ Parenting will be weakened and isolated: parents need tutors and tutors need parents and the child needs both to work together alongside their in-tutor group support team of students

We return to the challenges posed on the first page of Chapter One. If we are to redesign the way schools organise a learning process, we need to note the following and understand the implications.

1. **Real partnership and involvement with parents as key information providers and teachers**
2. **A coherent approach to information and individuals (managing variation...whole child)**
3. **Reducing parent complaint demands and building quality in (process partnership)**

4. **Re-engineering of the front and back offices to prioritise the teacher/tutor role (process)**
5. **Rapid response to learning challenges and a redefinition of 'care' (tutor as axis of learning)**
6. **Innovation throughout the school not from the centre (trust through quality partnership)**
7. **Coherent end to end operations supporting learning throughout the school (process)**
8. **School-wide understanding of how the organisation operates as a process (new roles)**
9. **Understanding how teaching and learning improves via nurture (learning relationships)**
10. **More fun and leadership (joy in work)**

These are the descriptors we should expect to see in a mature culture based on Vertical Tutoring. In particular schools must understand

- ∞ How VT improves quality teaching and learning (process issues)
- ∞ How to truly 'care' (abandon pastoral care for total [learning] care)
- ∞ How to renew real parent partnership (front office work and deep learning conversation)
- ∞ How to build a learning process based on a front office system (vertical tutor-based)
- ∞ How to enable all children to become leaders and mentors (extending learning relationships)

It is possible to write books on each of these concepts and many have. Transforming management is not easy in schools that have become so ingrained with their long-standing system orthodoxies. Transforming management is not a process of simply changing working titles which is what we are witnessing nationwide, but one of changing hearts, minds and actions and that means appreciating how other organisations behave to become world class. Sadly, public service systems are not a model schools should consider. Such systems are bureaucratic and overly concerned with apportioning blame, setting targets and trying to inspect faults out. They induce fear and stop people working with joy. Transformation means that the Leadership Team must change its behaviour first. Vertical Tutoring is the way forward and we need to understand how it works and why, paradoxically, it ticks all of the 10 boxes above!

In particular, we have to change schools from being back office operations that are unable to properly support classroom teaching and learning to front office ones that can. At the moment back office personnel see themselves as supporting children, supporting learning, resolving issues, creating relationships between the school and external agencies, working with parents and so forth. These good people sometimes achieve high quality work but the opportunity for mistakes and delays is high and the degree to which teaching and learning is supported is at best messy and uncertain. Back office ways simply absorb huge amounts of managerial energy that need to focus directly on the process of learning relationships. Meanwhile, customers are returned by the school's subject departments to the school's pastoral teams as complaints and mistakes. It is the same in the US and most other western countries.

To build in high quality requires that all those working in back office support system (most of the school) stop seeing themselves purely as service providers propping up near unworkable support systems and understand that they are also customers and leaders. It is the customer that expects high quality and sparks system change. To achieve 1-10 above, everyone in the school has to be both a customer and a service provider and so do parents and students.

This changes the way we look at the school as an organisation.

In short, we are not culturally, politically and philosophically ready to change the design of schools because as a nation we are hung-up on curriculum coverage issues and we don't really believe we can have everything. It is a divided view. Virtually every 'reform' introduced backfires, increasing uncertainty, undermining parenting and destroying trust in schools. Before we can think about redesigning schools, there is a need to rebuild partnerships, stop interfering with schools and stop seeing children as victims to be molly-coddled but see them as people, powerful and full of potential.

All children can learn but our national obsession of a life without risk ruled by tortuous regulation and an overly elaborate obsession with fairness, prevents schools from being creative and finding learning pathways that work. It always seemed to me as a Head that there was always a great solution to a child's learning and development blocked by a regulation. In over-protecting children, we have institutionalised the worst abuse of all: learning abuse.

Welcome to the ants' nest.

The problem with books is that they are sequential and this makes the discussion of models difficult. To appreciate VT and the values that drive it and the learning relationships it builds, there has to be an understanding of why organisations get stuck and why the route to better teaching and learning must take a detour via the tutor. To get to how VT is applied in practical terms requires an understanding of how schools operate and an understanding of why they behave in the way they do: the small schematic below indicates the route and is set against wider organisational theory. In this sense, schools are no different from other organisations and it is to organisational behaviour that we now turn.

It should be no surprise that ants are making a real comeback in films and could well be winning Oscars in the future. Let's face facts; ants have been around far longer than schools so we should not be surprised by their success as an organisation. How is it, Belbin (1996) asks, that ants have cracked so many of the prevalent problems of organisations that human beings have been unable to resolve? He helpfully offers us a guided tour: schools to the left, ants to the right.

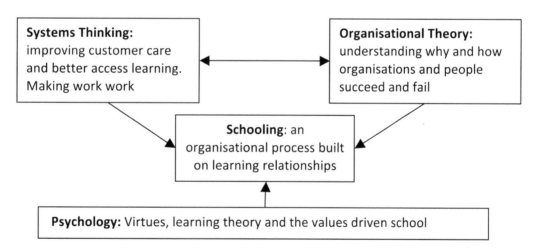

Figure 7: Route map for VT

Table 4: A Comparison in Features of Organisations: Humans v. Insects

	HUMAN	INSECT
Nature of Hierarchy	Centralisation. Individuals oversee and over-rule	Devolved nature of operations. Some individuals hold more vital jobs than others
Social Behaviour	Emphasis on individual gain	Focus on needs of community or colony
Communications	Top down. Junk material at other levels	Lateral, elaborate and multi-modal
Speed of Response	Delays due to single channel upward referral and intricate appeals systems in public sector	Rapid reaction force operating locally and containing the necessary specialisms
Source of Specialist Services	Extended education and training. Aptitude obscured by formal qualifications	Castes with genetically appropriate behaviour. Conversion of castes to meet perceived needs to situation

Ref: 'The Coming Shape of Organisations', R M Belbin 1996

Leadership

Belbin suggests that there are two fundamental principles to be learned:

∞ that there are better ways of running complex organisations than by making it the responsibility of a single boss

∞ that the larger the body corporate, the more important becomes the need for an organisation to be built around concurrent systems, differentiated in terms of function and scope, but interlinked rather than separated

Both points (above) work together and to a large extent describe the conditions for 'organisational transformation' and leadership: this is exactly what schools cannot do but think they do.

For schools the idea of 'distributive leadership' which seems to be vogue sees the need for leadership to be spread across the school; in a way, (the wrong way) it already is. TLRs (the way teachers are rewarded) and so-called *work force reform* prevent the spread of leadership and clog up much of what leadership there is in the school's back office, denying schools flexibility. This has resulted in an organisational flaw. The ants have a purpose to which all contribute. Their purpose is to pass on their genes. The purpose of the schools is less certain but tends towards achieving subject targets grades rather than developing human potential and this interferes with process and outcomes. The ants do have different roles but the process of feeding, breeding, fighting, heating, harvesting and maintaining combine to form a coherent and highly adaptable survival process honed over millions of years. Schools have a silo mentality so that when we add the idea of distributed leadership we tend to get separation rather than process. Thus any adaptation and change is very slow and difficult; schools get stuck on subject 'coverage', status issues and dependency delays and uncertainties.

The leadership concept sold to schools is highly limited and we end up with inappropriate models plucked from the sky such as 'Leading from the Middle' and an inadequate NPQH (presumably, 'Leading from the top'). The real key to leadership actually starts at the base of a learning organisation, in this case with the tutor. If the tutor is not the real *Leader of Learning*, a title wrongly bestowed on Heads of Year, the rest of leadership as a concept is unlikely to work well. It is the tutor who enables parents and tutees to be better leaders and it is at the base where the school can cash in because it is here where its massive reserves of leadership are banked. This clarifies the purpose of Headteachers and managers as builders of a learning process that (to continue the metaphor) releases and invests in such human capital.

Of course, ants are all related to each other and have behaviour genetically built in so it is not in their genetic interest to be too different and aspire to greater things. Schools need to adopt a similar approach whereby all who work in and around schools are seen as important leaders including parents, children, teachers, NTAs (incidentally, the daftest title in the school; how can you possibly work with kids and not be a teacher?) and especially the Headteacher. They must all contribute holistically to an organisational learning process and purpose beyond their own area. Tutoring especially, has become isolated from school purpose and any learning process. To be a successful organisation requires that everyone has an understanding of exactly how the school runs as a learning process so that all can play a full role in it and contribute.

Ants have no emotional attachment to the tasks they do. Teachers live out their working lives in school organisations that heavily influence their approach to the tasks and challenges they face. If the school is run by exterior forces prescribing what people do and how, if these schools are also riddled with blame and uncertainty and a silo mentality, we can and should expect unintended consequences and this is what happens in all public sector operations.

If we add a third column to Belbin's, there appears to be much in common between ants and VT.

Table 5: Systems

HUMAN (command / control)	INSECT (evolutionary)	VERTICAL SCHOOL CULTURE (Systems Thinking)
Centralisation. Individuals oversee and over-rule	Devolved nature of operations. Some individuals hold more vital jobs than others	The vital jobs are done by parents, the tutors and the tutees. This enables the teachers to do theirs
Emphasis on individual gain	Focus on needs of community or colony	Needs of the school are to achieve as an organisation. To do this requires a focus on every customer
Top down. Junk material at other levels	Lateral, elaborate and multi-modal	One back office of junked material and communications is replaced by many front office services
Delays due to single channel upward referral and intricate appeals systems in public sector	Rapid reaction force operating locally and containing the necessary specialisms	The enriched and supported front office service reduces complaint demands allowing more rapid response to others
Extended education and training. Aptitude obscured by formal qualifications	Castes with genetically appropriate behaviour. Conversion of castes to meet perceived needs to situation	The process and organisation does this by making everyone a leader, a learner and a teacher capable of responding and drawing down services

Ref: 'The Coming Shape of Organisations', R M Belbin 1996

If Belbin is right, we should expect to find evidence of hierarchy preventing decisions, material *junked* on others, delays and a general inability to provide and draw down appropriate services. We should also find high complaint demands, itself evidence of broken customer partnership.

The pastoral paradox

A good example of such organisational distortion is seen in what schools and Ofsted perceive to be their great strength: *pastoral care*. Here, the system intention is to remove barriers to learning but the consequence is to add to existing barriers. Many schools swear that without their system of pastoral care, their school could not function. Systems Thinking says the opposite is the case. Let's be clear; the traditional pastoral care system, year-based, runs as well as it can and those trying to make it work perform minor miracles. However, there is another way.

According to Ofsted, pastoral care is very good in schools except that none of it actually works effectively as far as building a learning process is concerned. Of course, schools think that their system of care does! Most schools have a pastoral system (Year Teams) and an academic system (Teaching Departments) broadly separated from each other. One side (the academic teams) appears to eventually *'junk'* work (a child not behaving appropriately in class) on the pastoral side (Head of Year / pastoral team). The child goes deeper into the back office system of the school which he/she can quickly learn to manipulate or become dependent upon over time. The system aim is to sort out the (behaviour) problem and recirculate the student back to the classroom and so on.

Such a model of managing personnel problems like a disruptive or vulnerable child is fraught with complications, delays and risk. The only person who ends up understanding the school's complicated back office system of managing such challenges is the child, who quickly learns the 'soft touches', communications weaknesses, inherent delays and where the information dumps are. The idea of *joined-up services* is so complex and time consuming that it is fraught with bureaucratic difficulty. This particular child becomes the system manipulator and the systems manager and is (paradoxically) the same child likely to fail at GCSE! Here is the true King of the Back Office and the main victim.

In fact, the idea that subject teachers 'dump' children they cannot cope with into the catch-all pastoral domain (the Head of Year in the UK, the school counsellors in the US, or monitors in France) is actually false although all schools seem to think it true. What is happening from a Systems Thinking view is something more subtle and entirely different. It *'appears'* to be the case, that this behavioural divide is the preferred method used by schools to manage more extreme classroom challenges. Heads of Year (HOY) often complain bitterly when a subject teacher sends a misbehaving child to them. They may even plead that they are not HOYs anymore but *'Leaders of Learning'*. What is happening is actually the opposite of what schools think is happening.

What is really happening is that children reach classrooms whereby both they and the teacher are unprepared and unsupported. The pastoral system has failed because of our conception of how it works (repair shop) is wrong.

The year-based pastoral system, instead of supporting learning as a process as should be the case, is actually the prime cause of teaching and learning difficulties in the classroom. The next chapter id devoted to tutoring and details what is going wrong. In essence the Head of Year is trying to do the job of the tutors who have been prevented from doing their work. If the pastoral side was proactive rather than reactive, especially in managing the support needs indicated by variation, teaching and learning would be easier for all. In this respect, it is the pastoral system that sends children to the classroom unprepared (learning relations unformed) and it is the pastoral system that *'dumps'* children into the learning system, not the other way round. The Head of Year is actually a *'super secretary'*, hugely overworked amazingly able but destined to lead a life of high stress.

Our schools have responded to targets and the inclusion agenda by building their systems the wrong way round and this creates learning obstacles and operational dysfunction on a grand (if accepted and largely hidden) scale. In this case, it starts with the poverty of tutor time, now reduced to a damage limitation exercise at the all important start of the day, and deteriorates as a support process from there. The child's behaviour is not addressed and appropriately supported on entry by tutors in any coherent and manageable way. It is not just a question of giving a tutor *'time to bond'* on the first school day in September; it is knowing how lasting learning relationships form and this does not mean a combination of admin tasks, circle time and SEAL! Children then become part of the dark mystery of the back office. It is teachers, armed only with an *individual action plan* from the Special Needs Department (or whatever name they now have) who are often the first to discover challenging behaviour in real terms and rightly wonder how this got through quality control; so a child gets sent back for some kind of behavioural treatment from the busiest person in the school.

Ofsted then makes the situation worse and praises schools to the heavens for pastoral work and it is true that there is no lack of effort to support children, except that it is the wrong effort delivered in the wrong way by the wrong person in a system upside down. Teachers are then open to criticism because of an apparent failure to *'engage children in learning'* even though tutors and teachers are the same people. So how does this all come about because it makes no sense? Complaints about behaviour remain high. Increased short term exclusions from schools mask permanent exclusion figures. Special schools have been replaced in school by Inclusion Units, itself in part a government inspired system of learning abuse and managerial incompetence. The big system requires constant repair and tinkering; new bits added to old; growing back office bureaucracies held together by sticky red tape.

This also reflects the degree to which school inspectors seem to lack any real idea of organisational learning theory (as opposed to what happens in classrooms), Systems Thinking and end-to-end operational process management. Instead of building in quality at the customer interface, we build in the potential for failure and schools don't see that the system being used doesn't work and cannot be made to work despite the nobility and sheer magnificence of their efforts.

Back to Hogwarts, the Tutor and the Tutee

On entry to Hogwarts, there is careful allocation to Houses which involves the magic of *'The Sorting Hat'*. This is a far more sensible way to allocate children to groups, other ways being far too risky. Schools have tried many of their own 'hocus-pocus' ways except the spells don't work and the magic is assumed (discussed below).

The breakdown of the system of pastoral management begins when the new intake arrives on day one of entry to a secondary school with a whole mass of assumptions regarding learning relationships and particularly the relationship between the tutor and tutee. The plethora of activities, procedures, learning packs and systems that schools use to 'support' the tutor actually undermine the tutor and fail the tutee. Schools have not adapted to the personalisation demanded in the third millennium and add to the growing separation between generations while thinking they are building learning bridges. This is explored in detail later (see Induction). Meanwhile, look closely at the right hand column (above) and consider the role of the tutor. Schools too often think they actually fulfil Systems Thinking descriptors of support and this is a real challenge if you have never known anything but the regurgitated and out of date methodologies that schools currently use and are reluctant to relinquish.

Of course, ants have had more time to learn about running organisations than schools have, and unlike schools, they rarely tolerate too much outside interference. They believe passionately that autonomy, teams and contribution should be functionally coherent and any capability genetically rewarded. They share with teachers a lemming-like willingness to sacrifice themselves for the greater good and to do whatever is asked of them without question even to accepting the blame when things go wrong. Ants also know that like schools, destiny and change is not high on their day to day agenda but survival is. Both cope differentially with variation and are passionate about the jobs they do. Yet, in so many ways, both teachers and ants are prisoners of old culture. For schools it is 100 years of old political thinking, for ants it is millions of years of adaptation and fine tuning.

There is another difference. The ant colony has evolved a system that can cope with most challenges. It evolves and adapts because all in it are part of a single survival process, free from conscious thought and marked by independent systems management: Darwinian system design in-built and shaped by evolution. Human systems are directed by rational thought and the systems we create are always a compromise, but they don't have to be the way they are; human systems are paradoxically slow to adapt to the rate of change we create and so require constant attention. School systems are invariably behind the curve but don't have to be.

In an ant colony, any defective labour is dispatched. This is what schools have erroneously done to tutors and this is where we go next.

If there is an education debate as opposed to a state implementation plan, it appears to revolve around the challenges of curriculum development, school leadership and teacher failure. So much has gone wrong that each is seen to be somehow at fault and this has deflected attention from the way schools manage learning and learning relationships as an end-to-end process. In fact, the education debate should concentrate on two key and interconnected areas: the first is reducing centralisation and allowing schooling to be decided by the dubious competence of a small clique, and the second is the whole business of school management and leadership in building effective learning organisations. The two are connected by trust or lack of it.

Having established a view that may horrify some schools; pastoral care as a back office system of customer repair rather than as preparation and support for a learning process, it is possible to go deeper into schools and explore what is left of the domain of the tutor. To understand Vertical Tutoring, it is first necessary to understand what has gone wrong with learning as a process and why the education debate so readily judges teachers and school leadership to be at fault. There is fault and most is self inflicted and relates to the way the system operates at a macro level: VT can only put this right (implement a plan) once we see what is wrong (the checking part). For secondary schools, it starts at one of the most critical times in the life of a learner, entry to secondary school.

Irony and the strange case of the Form Tutor and the school processing plant

When a child joins a (secondary) school, a *'process'* follows. A primary liaison team (the SENCO and/or Learning Support person, Head of Year 7 et al) prepare the way by finding out as much as they can about the individuals joining the new school. Liaison visits follow for students and parents to learn about the receiving (secondary) school and so ease the transfer process. Children are allocated to their tutor groups, their Year and their House. Later, they will receive their timetable and be allocated to classes. Throughout this process, good intentions are compromised by a whole series of management and learning assumptions reflected in orthodox practices that are dated, inappropriate and risky as far as induction goes. Of particular concern is the treatment meted out to a child's form tutor in the name of good practice and it is this *practice* that impacts directly and negatively on the school's ability to support a child's engagement with learning and the workings of the front office. **Few schools realise that what they do at this point can damage the school irreparably below the water line, or debilitate the school's effectiveness to a degree that requires all of its human resources to recover. In effect, what the school does in the first few days of the September term when new pupils enter the school and how it engages and supports them in learning will be a major determinant of the school's success.**

The irony is this: of the hundreds of schools that it has been my good fortune to know, all describe the front office (the domain of the tutor, the parent and tutee) to near perfection but none have been able to make it work properly despite the (wrong) effort put in on day one. Most LTs assume that their transfer system works when it palpably does not; most have undermined its value and how it should operate:

some don't know why it is there at all and others have reduced the tutor's role to an exercise in administration and registration (damage limitation). It is an area that horizontally (Year System) managed schools cannot make work per se. However, the culture of Vertical Tutoring relies on high quality tutoring (and so do parent partners and tutees) and sees this as the critical moment to build in value and establish loyalty groups capable of supporting and engaging with learning.

Induction

During an induction process (junior to secondary) schools with year systems (and too many of those wrongly claiming to be vertical) tend to have variations of the following with regard to the tutor.

1. The tutor may or may not meet their specific Y7 tutor group in the summer term (Y6) of induction.
2. Usually 'an opportunity' is given for the tutor to meet parents of Y6 en masse as part of the induction process for (say) 15-30 minutes to answer questions and run over school systems.
3. On the first day of term, tutors may have anything between two hours to a whole day with their tutor group. They will receive information about tutees on a 'need to know' basis from the Learning Support manager and/or from the Head of Year and will be given a pack to guide the day's administration and activities.
4. Tutors may be expected to teach PSHE or SEAL to their tutor group which most will do badly using packs if provided
5. Tutor time will be at the start of the day for 10-15 minutes followed by a short 5 minute session at the start or end of the afternoon session
6. There are 24-30 students in a tutor group.

Schools should be fairly familiar with the above. Macho schools will admit all students en masse to demonstrate their control and student compliance. Part of the claimed aim of the above is to establish the mentoring and advocacy 'bond' between tutor and tutee (a learning relationship). Unfortunately, nearly all of the *'settling in'* and *'getting to know each other'* practices (and those above) tend to do the complete opposite. For a child brought up in western culture it is most unlikely that any bond or learning relationship will develop through the induction process that schools practise, and schools don't see it. Schools think that because an outstanding tutor can make the induction system (above) work, everybody should be able to. In every one of the six bullet points above, the potential for damage to learning is unacceptably high and the assumption that some kind of 'relationship' develops is about as uncertain as it gets. Learning relationships are borne out of one to one and small group interactions, not circle time and admin.

If, however, we could get this bit right and understand how to form a tutor/tutee learning relationship further operational processes follow quite naturally, but this cannot be done in Year systems where time management issues intervene and where the values of family life cannot be supported and replicated in a meaningful organisational way. Bespoke learning relationships between the tutor and the tutee require very different thinking and management skills to that which is naively assumed and practised by schools. Our problem is that the factory notion of schooling we have gets in the way and so does regulation (the school as childminder).

As things stand, all of the above is detrimental to building the most critical learning relationship of all and, shows a disregard for the role of the tutor and the care of the tutee, no matter how schools dress up the above as good practice. The Leadership Team undermines the tutor and the whole school and it begins with the management misconception around tutoring. This starts on day one and worsens from that point. At best, tutees will end the first day with the view that their tutor is in charge of admin, is boring and is destined to play no significant role in their learning life. The system will, however, allow schools to tick SEF boxes but that is all and remains a factory style system for classes rather than for complex, individual youngsters, high in variation. This key relationship should establish the school's front office on which all other operational learning support processes of the school hinge. Poor practice (the case nationwide) here means that

a) The school cannot innovate
b) High quality cannot be built in and
c) Learning outcomes are put at high risk and especially so for the most vulnerable
d) Teaching is made difficult because learning relationships were not formed and the children ill-prepared and supported

Because some tutors are brilliant enough to make such a risky induction exercise vaguely appear to work, does not make it right. The claims of schools *to care* are bogus; values have been subverted and no learning process put in place. Having undermined the tutor as the true *leader of learning,* the Head of Year ends up doing the work that the tutor should be doing and soon a large back office system builds and things go from bad to worse as regulation increases in no time.

Meanwhile, here is the essence of all you need to know about running a school

∞ **The front office is THE Learning Gateway. Other 'gateways' mean nothing otherwise**
∞ **A child customer *'draws down'* services but cannot do so in a back office system (school)**
∞ **A child customer and family have to have their own, personal front office. This is the single most important entitlement needed to safeguard learning and build in quality**
∞ **The Year system is a back office system and Vertical Tutoring is a front office system and this management concept guides how a school operates and how learning becomes a coherent process**

Such is the macro system damage to school management and leadership thinking that schools may misinterpret these statements and rush off to build another special office with a special receptionist forgetting they already have these in place; broken, but in place; just. Schools have become so complex, so busy, so regulated, so off task, so centralised that their moral compass has wobbled erratically and they have ceased to be values driven, abandoned the idea of the *whole child* and have forgotten a simple theory of learning: the idea that it takes a whole village (extended school community and family) to raise a child. For parents, the school is the extended family and should behave as such. Again, this is not the direct fault of schools, but it is a system fault if schools do not recognise and address the situation by exploring vertical tutoring. All that is needed for organisational success and cultural change is an understanding of that very first building block, the cornerstone of the school's front office, how it works and why Vertical Tutoring is the one model that secures success.

But first, a survey: this survey is unique because the answers are attached. If you disagree with the answers, schools are not for you.

The first important questions about learning:

Question 1	Who is the most important person to a child as they enter a school?	
Answer	The child's tutor, that's who. Not the SENCO, not the Head of Year, not an LSA, not the Year 7 liaison person, not their best friend	
Question 2	Who is the key mentor and advocate of a child/student?	
Answer	The child's tutor, that's who. Not the Head of Year, not the SENCO, not the House Leader	
Question 3	Who holds the key to real parent partnership and customer services?	
Answer	The child's tutor that's who. Not other teachers or the LT or the Head	
Question 4	Who is the one person who should know the child well and can build in learning quality?	
Answer	The child's tutor, that's who. Not the SENCO, not the Connexions person, not the HOY	
Question 5	Who will tend to emotional intelligence and build self-esteem in students?	
Answer	The child's tutor, that's who. Not a SEAL or PSHE or citizenship teacher / programme	
Question 6	Who will ensure academic growth, access to learning and higher teaching standards?	
Answer	The child's tutor, that's who	
Question 7	When things go wrong who will always be there at the child's side?	
Answer	The child's tutor that's who and other kids in the tutor group	
Question 8	Who is the most undervalued, undermined, abused and most brilliant person in the school?	
Answer	The child's tutor, that's who	
Question 9	Who is the most underused resource and who should know the whole child best?	
Answer	The tutor, that's who	
Question 10	Who will always step into the breach when the tutor isn't there?	
Answer	The Assistant Tutor and the tutor group that's who.	

We know the answers to these questions because all schools seem to agree on these issues and all schools write it down in the tutor's job profile (below).

Parent Partnership

The tutor manages *the front office* because that is where the whole child is. It also satisfies a basic parent customer demand. Many parents say that all they want is for their child *to be happy at school*. Our system has reduced too many parents to this view but *'happiness'* has a more implicit meaning within a school context. It has also made many parents more challenging, more aggressive, more critical, more fearful and more uncertain, increasing back office demand complaints and system waste.

What parents really want as their child enters school is what schools promise to give: they want someone to be there for their child, someone to talk to, someone who will listen to their learning story, someone who knows their child well, someone who recognises *their whole child* and their child's potential, someone who will speak for the child and support his/her learning, someone that values parents and supports the family, someone capable of recreating the family in the school, someone who understands the back office and can make it work and someone who will always be there and keep in touch as needed. Later they want someone they know well to tell them how their child is doing and how, as parents, they can still be involved and valued, how they can help in difficult times, be better at what they do and have someone to tell them that they really are doing a great job. Systems thinkers call this 'customer services'. If schools are to be involved in a wider process of *social cohesion*, it begins and ends with the tutor and requires little in the way of regulation.

Ultimately, families want a healer and a guide through the moral maze and that is what the tutor does in a mature, vertically tutored school simply by being there and redefining what it is to really *care*.

It is the front office where the family draws down the services needed to make parents effective and it is the front office that makes teaching possible and student learning supported and effective. Current organisational practices do the opposite by breaking up and failing to recognise learning as a process and the possibility that everyone is a teacher as well as a learner.

The Keys to the Front Office and to Transformation:

All of this is the domain of the tutor. We cannot simply tick the parent box in a SEF and say, 'we've got a PTA' and a 'SENCO' and parent governors. The front office comprises the Tutor, the Child and the Parent. This is where parent partnership is made manifest and it is the front office that supports and dictates what the back office does. It is the front office that nurtures and supports engagement with learning, underpins and improves teaching and learning and which plays the critical role in raising standards and improving outcomes. It is the front office that has been destroyed by horizontal systems and target driven strategies that have caused massive damage to people, progress and the school as an organisation. It is this office and the tutor that is the real driver of innovation and transformation. It is the job of leadership and management to impact on the system to make the front office work work.

The front office at any given moment conceptually contains the tutor, a tutee, the parent and the rest of a vertical tutor group. This is precisely how and where high quality is best built in to a system like a school. In any given school, therefore, there will be as many front offices as there are tutor groups and as many different tutor groups as there are rooms.

Sadly, the critical role of the tutor in our schools is largely assumed and rarely properly supported. In essence, most schools inadvertently prevent and undermine tutors from effectively performing their advocacy and mentoring function. The point can be illustrated by looking at some common organisational practices. To rebuild the front office we need to understand how it came to be wrecked in the first place.

The Strange case of the form tutor's job profile

If we travel deep inside our schools and especially those with horizontal systems, we see that all schools share a broad view about the fundamental importance of the learning relationship between the tutor and the tutee, what some call an *'affect relationship'*. The following job profile is extrapolated from over 100 prospectuses.

- ◎ **To be the tutee's mentor**
- ◎ **To be the tutee's Pastoral Guide**
- ◎ **To be the tutee's Academic Guide**
- ◎ **To guide target setting processes with parents and tutee and use data and other information effectively in Academic Tutorials to improve outcomes**
- ◎ **To develop student Leadership and Citizenship**
- ◎ **To develop improved parental partnership**
- ◎ **To be the student's advocate**

What the job profile sets out is that first and most important learning relationship which underpins all others. These descriptors have to be established with great care, support and understanding of the school / customer relationship and need a very different approach to our complicated kids. The descriptors cannot exist as a set of vague beliefs and left to Heads of Years to apply; it is the fundamental role of school managers to convert such beliefs into working and operational reality because these are the most important activities in a school and the key to successful engagement with learning. **All teaching and learning depends on this.** Such a job profile (above) is a good description of the services provided in the school's front office. I have not come across a single school that does not try to deliver on these and I have never found one that operates a (year) system that gets remotely near. While schools are very good at the theory, the management practice (implementation) tends to fall well short of what it should be. In fact, too many schools manage these tasks in ways that are likely to have damaging consequences for staff, parents and pupils and on learning outcomes as they copy other schools and reinvent the past again and again. The irony is that schools try to do the best they can within the structures they have, but in reality there is almost a complete absence of any management and operational understanding of how learning relationships form or any real concept of how the separated component parts of schools should work together as a coherent learning process. Schools are not just separated by their internal silo teams but by an enforced external addiction to targets as outcomes. As has been said before, targets invariably change behaviour in bad ways: it is not that our schools have stopped thinking; it is that schools have been prevented from thinking.

The Systems Thinking blockage has its roots in Year Systems and can be traced back to 1965 and beyond and the erosion of House Systems. It is, in fact, the reason why comprehensive schools have never reached their full potential as organisations and it may well be that it is this failure that has caused governments to despair and then prescribe a medicinal overdose of regulation. There has been no theory of (organisational) learning to hold component parts together and Headteacher training has not progressed as much as it should. On day one of the NPQH, future Heads need to understand that Year Systems block effective learning management and the reasons why are set out throughout these pages.

The dreaded 'admin' word has been omitted from the job profile (above). When Systems Thinking is applied to current practice, it is clear that tutors are actually undermined by Leadership Teams from doing what it says on the job profile packet. If you are given a job to do with the wrong tools, the wrong time, no training and no understanding of the critical role you have to play in the operational structure, you really don't have a chance. If the children have also been badly prepared (inducted), the challenges double and it is all left to the teacher and this is wrong!

Most tutors are then undervalued because only the brilliant tutors can perform when all tutors should be able to. Schools say to me almost without fail how concerned they are about many of their tutors and their capability. They say we cannot go vertical because this means even more tutors are needed. They fail to see that it is not the tutors who are failing but the managers.

It gets worse. Lack of confidence in tutors and tutoring causes tutor time to be reduced to a damage limitation exercise. It gets worse. Pupils can now go through the school without ever having a meaningful conversation with anyone and so can parents. It gets worse. The students learn that the tutor does not really matter and is of little consequence. It gets worse. The kids take guidance from their peers and that can be risky. It gets worse. The tutor, after being undermined and devalued, is then expected to be a high quality teacher. It gets worse. Kids simply '*do*' school rather than enjoy school. And so the dreadful cycle goes on and on, decade after decade. All of the centralist intervention is rendered useless: external dressings for internal bleeding. We need to take our eyes away from the classroom and look hard at the point of entry to the school where families and tutors are and where the many front offices that should be the innovative and creative places where learning begins, lay abandoned and broken by school leaders: themselves broken by regulation, bureaucracy and a warped ideological view of how to build a safe and cohesive society.

Instead of supporting our tutor we have created a system that is designed to undermine any meaningful front office activity. If a school was to build in blockages to prevent effective tutoring, they might do the following: most do

1. **Ensure that the tutor group is year- based: this requires astonishing tutor / leadership expertise that very few have and build support systems that cannot work effectively**
2. **Ensure that there are 25/30 students in a tutor group and call this ethos. Make meaningful one to one and small group interactions between tutor and tutee as difficult as possible. Let the kids be with friends because that is what is important.**
3. **Make any meaningful dialogue between parents and tutors formally and informally difficult at 'meet the tutor' evenings and in 5 minute 'academic tutorials' and 'review days'. Call it 'settling in' liaison in Year 7 and target setting thereafter.**
4. **Give parents and students raw data and stats (rather than 'full' reports with comments) that they don't easily understand and cannot effectively use. Ignore the *whole child.* Ensure that the tutor receives minimal information about tutees, usually raw data and then expect the tutor or the kids to set meaningful targets**
5. **Make sure that tutor time is a high stress occasion involving uniform checks, homework checks, lateness checks, registration and communication of notices (admin time). Ensure that the tutor is seen as a low status peddler of information**
6. **Give 10/25 minutes for this task first thing in the morning and then repeat the whole sorry high stress affair for five minutes after lunch or at the end of the day. Ignore the fact that kids are often late and don't seem to value tutor time or the tutor**
7. **Ensure that tutors teach PSHE or SEAL (which most are pretty hopeless at) to their group because this makes some sort of pastoral sense... doesn't it? Assume that good learning relationships require a taught programme. Ensure that tutor time is not wasted through silly conversations. Give the tutor something to do like a tutor booklet, a tutor pack, a thought for the day, SEAL or PSHE. Time must be filled. No time for silly gossip**
8. **Ensure that the school compensates for the tutor's inability to deliver by building in support structures such as connexions, counsellors, HOYs, LSAs etc so that kids have someone less stressed to go to. A sort of pastoral safety net**
9. **Ask the Year Head to be the real tutor for 200+ students to give all the guidance needed because he/she is amazing and has loads of time for every child. Call her Leader of Learning**
10. **Assume throughout that parents are not needed and that learning relationships can form without individualised activity and leadership support from other students**

That should work OK! Having wrecked tutor time, we can then pile in other structures to prop up the one that has failed. Building on sand is always good: like towers in Venice. Nice but dangerous!

Of course this is a little facetious but it needs to be: it does, however, reflect the schools' approach to tutoring for too many years. The potential for harm to the individuals concerned, to the organisation and to learning is ignored because schools cannot innovate past blockages even if they recognise them; hence they have minimised the damage to (ironically) maximise learning. They have actually succeeded in doing the very opposite to what is needed. **It is perfectly possible for a tutee to go through a whole academic year without ever having a meaningful dialogue with their tutor or any other adult.** It also seems that children can go through schools without ever touching the sides because the distance between the tutor's job profile and any actualité is assumed and managerially and operationally undermined. Most schools do not even notice the damage because it is normal and accepted practice across schools and so assumed to be vaguely OK.

Such practices form part of the modern accepted orthodoxy whereby values have become confused or ignored and we have forgotten what it is to be human and what loco parentis really means. It is validated because some schools can actually make such a broken system appear to work but even in those schools where compliancy rules, if we look harder there is always a heavy cost paid by the 'whole child'. Surely, says the school, what is important is teaching time and the classroom. But to be effective, teaching time requires a direct conduit to the front office; without this, the teacher will be hampered from being world class. If tutoring malfunctions and it has, the tutor who is also a teacher finds herself on the back foot and school becomes dysfunctional: we start trying to repair the bit that vaguely works (teaching and learning) rather than the part that is completely shot (tutoring) upon which everything else depends. The quality of relationships in a school is critical and we ignore this truth at our peril. In particular, the tutor should play the single most important role in the school and by largely destroying that role, the rest of the operational processes malfunction, underperform and drift.

The sad nature of tutor time

It is precisely at the chaotic tutorial point where the school and the client base first interface that quality can be easily built in and real partnerships and learning relationships formed. Most schools do not see the opportunity and the moment is wasted at a huge cost to student learning and outcomes. Year systems are the root cause of this problem and should be replaced by Vertical Tutoring because this makes managerial sense with regard to service delivery. There is a vast difference, socially, academically and spiritually between a tutor group of 25 students all the same age and 18 students all of different ages with two tutors. One is largely about social control and driven by manager paranoia and the other is about care and support (nature and nurture) and driven by fun, leadership and real care. We might even call this 'citizenship'.

In most schools, we simply 'stress out' too many of our tutors and tutees at the very start of their day and then expect them to teach and learn as if nothing had happened. Students sometimes feel they can be '...a bit late to school because it's only tutor time!' The organisation devalues and undermines this most vital relationship because, in part, it wrongly believes that classroom teaching and learning is the single improvement focus and cannot see how dependent teaching and learning is on high quality tutoring. The connection between the teacher and the tutor (the same people incidentally) is ignored and assumed just as all other process relationships are. The tutors and their tutees are largely abandoned by the school to 'get on with it'. Parents are sidelined. Tutor time is often reduced to an exercise in damage limitation and filled with low priority tasks at low priority times. Learning relationships never form properly and the child is the worse for it because to him/her, the school does not seem to care. Many seek a kind face elsewhere and we are lucky that there are so many such faces in our schools. However, without a supportive tutor/advocate/mentor to recreate the family in the school, learning is diminished and the school as a system open to failure.

Schools pay a heavy price when they fail to appreciate how tutor/tutee learning relationships form. The socio-dynamics of the school can become dangerously out of kilter with many tutees hardly spoken to at all during their first crucial settling in year. In effect, schools create low level learning relationship opportunities and place tutor time in a low priority place in the school day. The tutees see through this relationship and tend to cope by relying on and learning from each other almost in isolation from an adult mentor. Peers can become a more powerful influence than tutors (and teachers by implication) and no-one is guiding the groups that determine learning and *openness to experience.* The school teaches this as part of the hidden curriculum of life skills and then attempts to counter process failure with PSHE and SEAL programmes. There are groups within groups and much as schools may refer to the importance of 'ethos' too many pupils/tutees are hurt, isolated and let down by the school system. In nearly every school there is hit and miss management in hit and miss systems. **The tutor can never be the person that the tutees need him / her to be. There is no parent partnership worthy of the name in UK schools. We build rigid systems on unstable learning relationships and vague assumptions and only get away with it because those who work in our schools are so magnificent and we think of compliancy as a value.**

Chapter 9: Learning from Corporate Failure

Unless there is risk and a sense of transformation, schools as organisations become moribund and dependent. Unless they learn from and work with customers (especially parents) they cannot build quality in. Unless everyone is involved in and understands what a process is and the part each plays in it, there is no incentive to improve and get better. Unless we can give back more autonomy to schools and individuals, they cannot earn trust and be innovative. Failure should be a great teacher but what school systems do is repeat mistakes that can be rectified at zero cost.

Regime Change

I have come across many schools where Heads have been deemed to have failed and a new regime put in place to take over the school. It usually follows a critical Ofsted or two and somebody somewhere says 'the school needs shaking up' or 'there's too much deadwood'. I remember a Chair of Governors saying to me on taking up my second Headship, 'You'll need to shake a few branches, here.' He never actually said what might fall out of the tree if I did. As soon as I started even looking at the branches, even from a healthy distance, the whole of the governing body went into a synchronised tail spin of uncertainty spurred on by staff who thought they might have to change what they do. No-one actually says specifically what is really organisationally wrong beyond the identification of 'under achievement', 'drift' and some vagaries of leadership. 'Regime change' is always a popular pastime with western governments. It starts with the folly of 'shock and awe' and the assumption that the pieces can be picked up and that all will be well. The new boss usually re-labels the Leadership Team with new titles that cover all the required management bases and such new energy, uncertain as it is, helps the organisation improve by concentrating on learning rather than ideology. The former Head retires or moves on. However, school failure is more complex: we need to know what it is that has really gone wrong and why governors should share the support burden of leadership more than they do.

Perhaps, if Heads received support, training and advice beyond the SIP (school improvement partner) and superficial Ofsted targets, Heads might be more effective.

When school employees understand their customer and service provision roles the operational organisation of the school is more likely to be successful in delivering better services. It survives and thrives. To really appreciate the need for substantive cultural and organisational change, schools first need to reach a point where they understand where the delivery blockages are. The pastoral system is a key area; time is another, Workforce Reform, TLRs and curriculum another and so on. This is hugely problematic for school managers and leaders because what they often consider to be strengths (e.g. the pastoral system, care, support for teaching and learning) are actually process weaknesses (discussed above). Educational ideas and management assumptions simply collide and confuse; it is as if learning and running a school have become incompatible except in the slang of education speak.

To underpin the need for change we need to understand why organisations fail. Shukla takes us into the area.

Table 6: Understanding Corporate Failure: M. Shukla (1996)

Reasons For Corporate Failure	Underlying Learning Disabilities
1. Life-Cycle Decline	Inadequate environmental scanning, and internal competency-building
2. Trapped by Past Success	Complacency and arrogance leading to rigidity and lack of openness to new knowledge
3. Inappropriate Strategic Biases and "Mental Models"	Lack of self-critiquing and self-reflection causing misalignment with the environment
4. Rigidity in Response to a Crisis	Defensive and self- destructive routines and practices hampering adaptive responses

It should now be easy to understand the nature of these *disabilities*. These descriptors herald (in the private sector at least) the demise of old paradigms. The life cycle comes to an end when the system becomes moribund and cannot respond to, meet or recognise new customer demands. This not only applies to schools but to all their disparate system parts and sister institutions. However, the approach to schools is not to let them go out of business but to further complicate existing moribund cultures with new *'fixes'* in the shape of new reforms, new rights and new initiatives. The underlying culture remains the same. In other words, central interference makes any 'underlying learning disabilities' worse. Shukla's four points strike home with unnerving accuracy especially when applied to our schools and not just those in special measures or under *National Challenge* to improve. It is worth taking a little time on each of the above.

Life Cycle Decline: as the social and learning demands on schools increase so the organisation must evolve to deliver more complex services (inclusion, ECM agenda, sex education, careers, Diplomas etc) and this requires transformation of the key management operations and tasks. However, we are not quite sure what the core purpose of a school is anymore as they vacillate to meet ever changing academic and social directives using the same basic internal systems and personnel already tied in by pay structures and so-called workforce reforms. What is plain to see is the management skills gap between the high ability of school employees and the processes they must use to support learning, effect change and improve outcomes. Because a school's operational practices have remained *rigid* the school's internal management competencies have not developed to meet demands and remain largely unchanged. Titles change and job descriptions increase. There is a contradiction here because teaching has definitely improved; teachers have just about maintained standards despite ever increasing social demands, on-going and ill conceived curriculum change and an internal school structure that fails to properly support teaching and learning in a coherent way. They are truly heroic. However, such a state of affairs is untenable. We end up with all the right people doing the wrong jobs in the right place in the wrong way. This leverages the politics of centralisation rather than innovative internal transformation. In many respects our schools are operationally well past the point of *life cycle decline* and require urgent rethinking. The tragedy is that with schools, life cycle decline is a permanent feature of organisations that have to play catch-up with an innovative centre.

Trapped by Past Success: this is a major challenge for our schools and especially so for our 'good' schools. 'Good' schools appear to be OK and become some kind of management and operational role model of best practice for other schools and this can be a big problem. We might incorporate struggling schools into Trusts under a new executive Headteacher. This can be helpful and unhelpful. It can serve to offer the illusion to other schools that current management methodology is OK and can actually work when the opposite is the case. It also tells schools that a cultural change like Vertical Tutoring can be somehow incorporated into the existing management system as a tool for school improvement or as a token change to a pastoral system. Complacency is a problem but 'ignorance and arrogance' more so. Passing on broken systems between schools simply recreates orthodoxy and the illusion of improvement and this is what the SSAT and NCSL tend towards when they offer mass training opportunities. This is after all what compliance leads to; the illusion of change. Rather than spring the trap of orthodoxy we simply keep resetting it, and forget it is there until we walk into it again and again. Teachers no longer seem to notice the pain and have developed ways to cope. Past success can lead to drift while copying what is seen as best practice is problematic.

Inappropriate Strategic Biases and 'Mental Models': schools find it difficult to reflect (check the system out for faults). They are all about action and filling time so that reflective time-outs are rarely called and as valued as they should be. The mental model is governed by tick-boxes and compliance to inspection. The system is anti-time while pretending to be pro-time. Unless the beliefs held by a school undergo external management critique (something Ofsted is either not yet competent enough to do or not allowed to do) the way a school operates can so easily be based on assumptions rather than made manifest and this is highlighted below. It is almost impossible for schools to 'check' their own Systems Thinking because

- ∞ **The style of the SEF is superficial and inappropriate. It is simply a checklist of compliances**
- ∞ **Thinking has been heavily institutionalised over many decades**
- ∞ **The language of education is unsafe and inaccurate for school managers**
- ∞ **Work is geared to achieving external targets and not delivering high quality services**
- ∞ **Ideology changes every ten years as one government takes over from another**
- ∞ **Dependency means no internal substantive checking is warranted. Questionnaires are not an answer as system thinking clearly states.**

There is also a lack of genuine management training for headteachers and others. In Langford and Cleary's (1995) 'fable', they tell of a school that had pioneered process ideas (based on Deming) and was transforming the way it operated. As word spread, schools tried to copy the system but they only saw the superficial bits (lesson length, grading, assessments etc). Each thought that this would bring the quality components needed by their own school. *'They were wrong'*. We can see this today with Heads returning from all over the world with their magic answers to *the school problem*. All miss an important point about learning relationships and a complete understanding of Systems Thinking approaches. At least they try.

Rigidity in response to a crisis: there are many system rigidities, most of which go largely unrecognised by Leadership Teams. These (listed below) would be encompassed within and accompanied by innovation in normal working environments. Among them are parent partnership, the Year System, the pastoral system, curriculum coverage allocation, inspection, assessment and so forth. All are rigidities rather than innovations (Diplomas have the effect of making timetabling and school days stuck fast) and are more likely to keep the school as an organisation the same. This makes crisis management a common organisational feature rather than a rare one, as the same underlying process faults fail to adapt to changing system and cultural demands. Other systems brought in to deal with a crisis tend to be hypercomplex (over-regulated), over-sophisticated, unworkable, unaffordable and invariably add to system overload. Joined up thinking and services are rarely joined up because they contain time and communication challenges that are not easily resolved. The partnerships and teams needed in a crisis cannot operate quickly and effectively as each follows their own back office procedures, timetables, priorities and audit trails: the need for decisions is delayed and responsibilities confused and all of this is further hampered by the fear and increase of mistakes that bureaucratic processes create.

It is helpful to apply Shukla's Chart to schools.

Table 7: Why Schools fail (adapted from Shukla)

Reasons For School Failures	Underlying Learning Disabilities
1. Life-Cycle Decline	Schools do not work effectively with customers (student and parent) and appear to have actually distanced themselves from parents. Schools claim otherwise. Year structures prevent partnership and teaching support. Teaching competency is seen as deficit and non-teaching staff shoehorned in to repair back office systems. This is partly the result of dependency culture and a failure to innovate at the point of customer (student) need. In effect, schools continue to employ systems no longer fit for purpose. Motto: *'It will all come round again. It always does.'*
2. Trapped by Past Success	Schools reach a plateau where leadership complacency and/or arrogance cause drift. Any change is superficial .The same moribund culture continues unabated. There may even be open hostility to change caused by previous bad experiences. There is a lack of openness to external advice. Past success prevents future adaptation. There is a tick-box culture. Motto: *'We know best and what works for us. Ofsted said so!'*
3. Inappropriate Strategic Biases and "Mental Models"	Schools know that their systems don't quite work so they work on ones that vaguely do but are unable to fix the rest. Managers cannot see that there are other solutions because thinking and reflection are impaired by survival and compliancy tasks. They ignore what is wrong and quickly become misaligned with their stated aims and values. Motto: *'I don't have to think anymore, therefore I am not!'*
4. Rigidity in Response to Crisis	As decline sets in, the old systems cannot cope and neither can the managers. The many policies don't quite work and over-regulation adds rigidity. Complaints are not dealt with and soon things get serious. Defensive and self- destructive routines and practices hamper any adaptive response. Motto: *'Wait and see; it will all come out in the wash!'*

Such organisations have no single reason for falling short of delivery expectations and it is apparent that a number of systemic factors contribute to failure. What is clear is the impairment of an organisation's ability to encourage and release creativity (*'to learn'* in Senga's terms) that is most at risk and as Clegg and Birch (1998) said, *'Creativity is all about breaking with the past'.*

Before we examine schools *close up and personal*, a final detour is needed. Charles Handy has always made sense of the world of organisations. Time to ride the sigmoid curve...

Life on the Sigmoid Curve

All organisations and our lives follow a pattern of waves. We live out our lives facing good times and bad. Life for individuals and for organisations really is *'a box of chocolates'* as Forrest Gump said. Schools as organisations are no exception. They lead an organisational life that has its ups and downs. Each seeks to improve and reach point 'A' (Fig: 9). This is an elusive but key marker for schools. It is a time when there is a sense of achievement and when news is good. It is also a time when one cultural way of doing things can no longer take the school forward. Here, there is a danger of Shukla's corporate disabilities (and especially the *ignorance and arrogance* hypothesis) coming into their own. At point 'A', schools tend to say one of two things

1. We have got the exam results as high as we can. We seem to have done all we can within the constraints we have. What next?
2. We are a good school. Ofsted say so. We should continue the way we are: 'If it ain't broke, don't fix it!'

The first school acknowledges its current success but recognises the need to embrace further changes if it is to maintain upward momentum. They often have no idea what this might be but they continue to scan their environment for clues, listen at the periphery for system noise and recognise the danger of organisational inactivity. It is willing to ask and is open to Systems Thinking scrutiny though not from a SIP, the LA or Ofsted (likely to embed old ideas). The second school is *'arrogant and ignorant'* to use Shukla's words and will continue to absorb change and bolt bits on to its existing management platform. Such schools only listen to the centre or copy other the practices of other schools and end up drifting.

At Point 'A' (fig. 8 below) organisations are at a crossroad and things can get stuck. There is a performance plateau. Life is becoming complex as social, cultural and learning demands and challenges increase

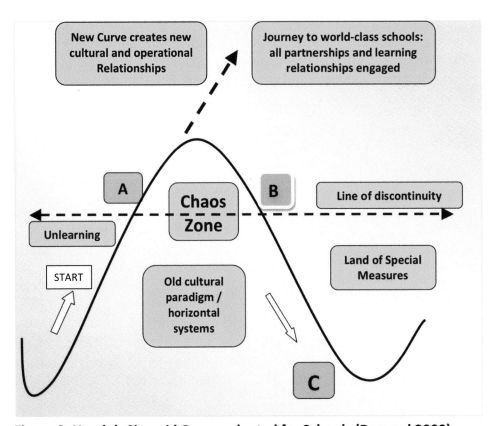

Figure 8: Handy's Sigmoid Curve: adapted for Schools (Barnard 2000)

requiring new thinking. At an emotional intelligence level, it marks a point between feeling confident and excited by the challenge and being complacent or overwhelmed. The former allows the possibility of movement forward and the latter endangers the whole school as an organisation.

Life at Point A

At point 'A', the news is good. Exam results are up, parents like the school, the last Ofsted was good, staffing is stable and all seems reasonably well with the world. The school thinks it is coping with system demands and feels confident and successful.

But we know that organisations are fragile and it is all too easy to drift and fall if left unattended. The school has got this far with their old factory system, now computerised with new personnel drafted in to plug the back office gaps. Members of staff have worked hard to make things work and to get where they are at Point 'A'. But it is precisely at this point where news is positive and morale is high that the school is at its strongest and is best equipped to break with the past and create a new culture. However, there is confusion. One of our schools thinks it should simply continue doing what it does (arrogance and ignorance = complacency). The other knows it should do something but is unsure what that might be (anxiety and excitement = uncertainty) but is willing to embrace the challenge of motivational theory.

Point 'A' sits on a line of discontinuity that separates cultural paradigms. These lines can appear anywhere and at any time that major change is called for. Here, the aim of the game is to maximise the creative energy available within the school to enable it to assess its practice and learning process and so create a new sigmoid curve. The old ways are abandoned. It is a point of transformation and the challenge here is *'learning to unlearn'*. It means throwing off the shackles of institutionalised learning, bureaucratic year structures and endless targets to embrace the good chaos of endeavour, joy in work and a world of endless creative opportunities offered by Vertical Tutoring, Systems Thinking and a new approach to school management. In effect, it is about strengthening learning relationships and school values.

At point 'A', simply copying other schools and trying DIY changes is unlikely to work. Such activity simply spreads system viruses by inheriting the organisational faults of others. Even DIY change takes skill and learning and the need to thoroughly understand the instructions on the packet. Unfortunately, all that is written on the Vertical Tutoring packet is a set of values and a manifesto for learning as a process that starts with relationships. For this book, Point 'A' marks the change from a horizontal culture of organisation to a vertical culture, from 'conveyor belt' to 'bespoke' and from just nature to nature and nurture. It is the only change, in my experience, that can enable schools to build in the high quality operational systems they need to underpin and meet new and increasing demands. It ensures that every child really matters and supports social cohesion. Point 'A' is the take-off point and the best opportunity for easy success. Life elsewhere is trickier.

Point B

Point 'B' sees the organisation plummeting downwards. The school has failed to recognise point 'A' as a time of change and saw it as a rest stop. Instead, it drifted over the curve and was unable to respond when the crisis inevitably hit. Falling backwards over a sigmoid curve is never pleasant and the black hole of special measures and National Challenge can easily await those that do. Any recovery is more difficult on the dark side of the curve. But even here, where life is organisationally under threat, the culture can be changed and a new course planned. The school still has more control than it realises even though change here is urgent. Here, the school must reassess, rebuild and find its upward curve. The difficulty here is leadership and energy levels but the imperative to change is greater (reality check has negated arrogance and ignorance).

Point C

At point 'C' change is not an option but is externally mandated rather than driven from within. This school needs help with Systems Thinking and they are, paradoxically, unlikely to find it from within the system that purports to support and partner them. Here, where confidence is low and energy drained, the school has to gather what strength it can and return to its core activities by constructing an upward improvement curve. If it fails to do so, it might easily disappear forever, be incorporated through regime change or made into an Academy.

Wherever a school finds itself, its forward journey cannot be just a question of simply applying its existing policies and practices with even greater rigour; there are other tools in the management box. All schools can completely overhaul what they do by checking their system (with help) and acting to change their culture which is what VT should enable. On day one of a change such as Vertical Tutoring, the school only needs a very few simple procedures in place but the effect will be immediate and life enhancing.

The great thing about sigmoid curves is their wormhole properties. School leaders can conjure them up whenever they are inspired to do so. It is simply a question of timing and knowing how they work and where to find them. Wormholes are, of course, vertical; they carry you up and take no time at all. When the Headlearner is ready, the teacher will appear and the wormhole will be revealed.

Let me end this chapter by reintroducing 'enterprise' (SS Enterprise that is) to the system. The task here is to discover which spaceship you are in and where you might be within the hyperspace of a sigmoid curve.

Let's Play 'School Trek'

Enterprise 1: this ship always had the most difficult route through the Asteroid Belt of Learning. It is never easy being at the helm when large meteors are being thrown at you from all sides by the space pirates from the evil Planet Ofsted. Life is not fair. The Captain and senior officers spend all of their time filling in the requisite Health and Safety forms and attending relevant safeguarding courses, besides plotting new directions as ordered by the DCSF (Directorate for Competency, Specifications and Form-filling). The LT is now too terrified to touch anything without direct orders from above. Besides, cynical crew members say they have done all of these journeys before and that there was nothing there the last time they went. One asteroid is bound to hit sooner or later, it always does. Life on board is not easy. Systems have pretty much broken down and the crew always seem to be on the verge of mutiny: many are being treated by the ship's doctor for stress and depression and replacement crew are difficult to find. The energy supply of dilithium crystals is running low and the ship is now pretty much marooned in space. The captain has barricaded himself in a bunker on Level 5 with a SIP who notices that among the few school awards on show is one saying 'National Challenge'; meanwhile some of the crew have abandoned ship. To make matters worse, a signal has been received from Planet Ofsted saying that their crack alpha inspection team is about to arrive. In the engine room, Scottie is shouting, '...the engine canna' take any more...' but then he always says that!

Enterprise 2: this ship too is pretty much in permanent orbit around Mother Earth and stays in close contact with the DCSF and the SSAT (Starship and Satellite Advancement Team). The captain (called CW by the first officer, R. Perrin) uses the transporter room to make frequent visits to conferences to ensure that he is seen in the right places and is up to date and compliant with any changes. His joy is being the first to show that he is in line with the latest central thinking of the Fat Controller Secretary of Space Cadets. He is rarely seen on board and visits other star ships to spread good practice, believing in a *hands-off* approach to captaincy. *'Stay in close orbit and nothing can go wrong'*, is his motto, *'don't want to take risks and damage the paintwork'.* Many of the crew suspect that he has been assimilated by the Borg. Despite being systems savvy, nothing really changes on board and policies and practices are impeccably maintained by the crew who prefer it when the captain is absent and the high ability No. 2 takes over. The crew feel safe but the ship is going nowhere and could easily fall out of orbit if there is a gravity shift or if a black hole suddenly materialises in the ship's accounts.

Enterprise 3: there is high satisfaction that the journey is going well. The captain, however, dislikes engaging Warp Drive, preferring a slow steady drift and a largely uneventful journey. *'Steady as she goes, Spock'.* Indeed she has no real desire to encounter new life forms and hardly understands the ones that form the crew, especially the Klingon, Worf. The crew tell a story about the time the Captain saw a UFO. It was at a filling station and actually had UFO written on the side. Fortunately Spock pointed it out that it stood for 'Unleaded Fuel Only'. Otherwise, the crew is undemanding and efficient. Everything complies with regulations. The distance from Mother Earth gives a false sense of security and independence This is the safest ship of all but semantics and words are a communications problem here. Once every lunar cycle, the young people on board attend a student voice class with the EMH (Emergency Medical Hologram) to complain about the Ship's toilet system. This ensures no decisions are made. And what was it that Spock said? Ah yes! *'Go 4th and prosper!'*

Enterprise 4: nobody knows where this ship is and any communication with central control at the DCSF is conveniently mislaid, misinterpreted or ignored by the maverick ship's captain who believes that all those at the Centre need brain transplant therapy (something he kindly offered to give them personally). Warp engines have been abandoned in favour of wormhole time travel and it is rumoured that the kids on board have taken over the helm believing it to be an X-Box. The crew seem to spend much of their time spaced-out on the holodeck where they imagine new futures and create better worlds. The captain's motto, *'Let it be so'* seems to work. Not only have they discovered a better version of chaos theory but they have also discovered a strange new life form to guide their way: they have given it the name, *'family'*.

Beam me up, Scotty.

Before taking the final leg of this part of the journey, a visit to the pyramids will remind us what schools do. There are some things in the past that are so fundamental to learning and values driven that they need to be retrieved and updated. We need to go back and reinvent

- ∞ Tutoring
- ∞ The academic tutorial (deep learning conversation)
- ∞ The House system
- ∞ Student as Leaders

...and the pyramids tell us why. They also help to explain how Vertical Tutoring works. The work of Abraham Maslow, the late humanist psychologist, is more relevant today than ever. Within Maslow's Hierarchy of Needs lie the foundations of Vertical Tutoring and the relationship needs that best enable and support learning.

Maslow's Hierarchy

Pyramids are old but they endure. They are a point of reference and provide us with a bridge to another age. We need to spend a little time in the past. Here, many of the principles and values of Vertical Tutoring can be found among the debris of forty plus years of the most mismanaged and misled education system ever seen. Only our amazing teachers and resilient kids shine through and continue to hold things together. Many teachers hark back and believe it was more fun then: in many ways they are right. Our new young bloods have learned to worship the empty and glib mantra that, *'It's all about teaching and learning'* and too often see this as a passport to early promotion and the illusion of transformation. The mantra masks the mysteries of the past and we attempt to build schools and academies with half thought out ideas rather than bricks and mortar. Few get it right.

What builders of pyramids know is that you start from a firm base. In schools, that base is the relationship between the tutor, the tutee and home. We have to believe and appreciate that there is nothing in a school that is more important. I have been to hundreds of schools and met more school leaders than I care to remember. They all believe this to be so. However, I cannot recall a single school that has truly supported tutor time in ways that underpin and really value tutoring as the single most important activity of the school, and the activity that if done well can do most to improve student outcomes.

Maslow's pyramid helps explain why it all went strangely wrong and what is necessary to put it right and he and gives clues as to what tutoring should be. Maslow helps us put things in context and shows us how to build a school.

As suggested above, when schools can gear the totality of their human resources into a process view of teaching and learning which is all joined up, magical things can happen. But to achieve this higher management state requires recognition that within many schools are critical relationships that may not be working in the way that we assume. There is almost too much pastoral care and yet, not enough

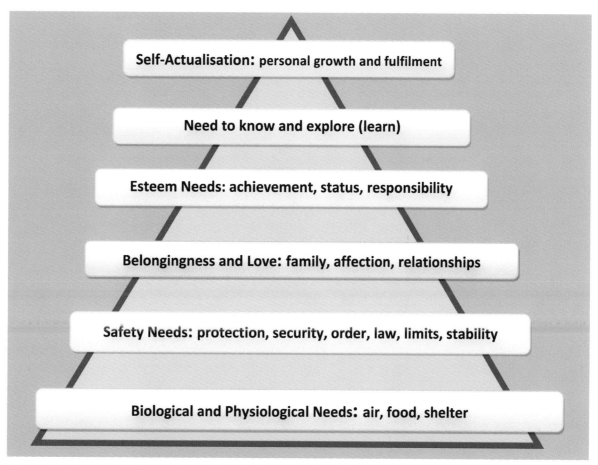

Figure 9: Maslow's Hierarchy of Needs (extrapolated)

'care'. We create patched-up systems for patched-up kids. As things stand, if we believe our social research, our society is in melt-down, loneliness is a major issue and our young people have the lowest self esteem in Europe. They are also the most likely to get pregnant, to fall foul of the law, to carry weapons, to join gangs, get drunk and take drugs. Yet, teachers know that most are also amazing and talented young people. Luckily we are also blessed with the most dedicated and hardworking teachers, so what's going wrong? How can we raise self esteem and create better learners at the impact point where the school and the family interface?

What the pyramid tells us is a very important truth with regard to the school as a system. For learning to take place, other needs have to be addressed and 'affect relationships' formed: those working in schools cannot be separated 'component parts' but must form part of an end to end process of learning relationships. The pyramid (above) is a blue print for VT which tells us that if we teach less and listen more, we learn more. VT works because it addresses needs that have too often been unattended, head on. It makes the school safe, it recreates the best of family in the school, and it raises self esteem through leadership training and opportunities and responsibility for others: it builds the platform that facilitates engagement with learning. This cannot be done and must not be attempted through teaching programmes alone, but through the learning relationships that tutoring extols as a virtue. The difference between teaching and tutoring will fade over time as the school builds confidence in the new system. It is a system of deep emotional intelligence (EQ) that will grow naturally into spiritual intelligence (SQ) over time.

It is nurture first. Any attempt to teach our way through needs using subject methodologies (PSHE, RE, SEAL, Sex Ed and Citizenship etc) may be heroic processes but make little sense to the most vulnerable and many others. All are fraught with institutional and pedagogical difficulty and do not seem to be as effective as hoped, and some may be counterproductive. They are bolted on to save us all. The school has to work together in a coherent way and deal with the whole child from the word go. Thus, citizenship is the way the school is run: when kids understand that citizenship is '*cool*', rewarding and requires leadership, we can teach and learn about citizenship. Relationships come first because relationships build trust and optimism.

This means resisting the pressures of social curriculum developers and the increasing hotch-potch of ideas and demands from pressure groups and un-thinking think tanks that stretch the capacity of schools to breaking point in the catch-all name of 'reform'. Education is littered with the discarded waste of such lost initiatives and the endless stream of failed system upgrades.

Education can never work unless we redefine what it to care and this takes us directly back to Systems Thinking and the way we run out schools. When schools are run from the base up, students, teachers, NTS (non-teaching staff) et al tend to have a very clear idea about a school's priorities. Set out below are some of the belief statements from Mt. Edgecumbe High School, Alaska. Management delivers on beliefs: the school is values driven. The ideology is 'Systems Thinking' and so stems directly from the work of Deming.

Our actions are based on the following beliefs

1. Human relations are the foundation for all quality improvement
2. All components of our organisation can be improved
3. Removing the causes of problems in the system inevitably leads to improvement
4. The person doing the job is the most knowledgeable about the job
5. People want to be involved and do their jobs well
6. Every person wants to feel like a valued contributor
7. More can be accomplished by working together to improve the system than by working individually around the system
8. A structured process using statistical graphic problem-solving techniques lets you know where you are, where the variations lie, the relative importance of the problems to be solved, and whether the changes made have had a desired impact
9. Adversarial relationships are counterproductive and outmoded
10. Every organisation has undiscovered gems waiting to be developed
11. Removing the barriers to pride of workmanship and joy of learning unlocks the true untapped potential of the organisation
12. Ongoing training, learning, and experimentation are a priority for continuous improvement.

Edgecumbe is a school much visited. It is also much copied albeit unsuccessfully by other schools. Few schools walk the talk of such principles and values because they fail to appreciate the process philosophy and human drivers that make Edgecumbe what it is; fun and successful. It has a set of beliefs and values that guide action and draw heavily on Deming's 14 points set out below. In England, schools invariably start with the idea of relationships but then get sidetracked by other priorities. With Edgecumbe, this is unlikely to be the case because the beliefs imply that this school knows much about management and what it is to really care about learning. Had I read this book and understood Systems Thinking when I started out, I might have been a great Headteacher.

School management as learning

No matter how the school as an organisation is operationally planned, good or bad, it will impact directly on how children, and especially the most vulnerable, engage with learning.

Put simply, engagement with learning is not just a facet of classroom management and the curriculum; it is a function of all school management. In particular, learning is not just a subject classroom activity: the real classroom is the school where we all learn and support each other. In many ways our teachers are on the receiving end of the operational system. While the subject classroom may be where most curricular learning occurs, the front office is where the school as an organisation ensures that individuals can draw down all that they need to prepare and support them; the vertical tutor group is Maslow's Pyramid and so is the school. It has to be solid, safe and lasting and the tutor runs the place in a way that makes students feel confident about engaging in learning knowing that nothing much can go wrong that cannot be put right. The nature of how schools deliver that support is a management issue of the highest and most pressing order, especially in our disconnected western culture. We are fortunate to have magical places and magical people walking the secret gardens of our schools and it is the function of leadership to build a system that best enables everyone to be of this kind.

Let us look again at our schools and make Maslow our Chair of Governors. Now let us try and apply the constructs he uses.

1. Basic Needs: at last we are rebuilding our schools and making them into places that kids can relate to. This is good. Academies often provide breakfast (and school uniform) at the start of the day. Apparently, one third of UK kids live in poverty (system failure). Those arriving at school unfed will struggle with concentration. Providing breakfast is such a sensible thing to do and probably does as much to enhance learning and teaching as anything else. Meanwhile we are hung up on school lunches

2. Safety Needs: arguably, our students are in most danger from their peers, unwanted peer pressures and Children's Secretaries. Schools tend to promote this unsafeness. This can take the form of very real physical and emotional damage. Anti-bullying, anti-knife and anti-drug policies and the like are only part of any counter strategy in an age when schools find it difficult to stop children from chewing gum. Our history of year systems and so called year ethos may well be the perfect organisational breeding ground for gang culture. Those who watch 'The Dog Whisperer' will know how we humans fail to understand the 'power of the pack' and leadership at peer level. Only vertical tutor systems can effectively change student relationships for the better and this is one of the most powerful influences we have to enhance learning. The school home link is also critical here in a world where parent partnership is preached and largely ignored at the same time

3. Belongingness and love: this begins in the home, so the school must relate closely to home through a much deeper shared information partnership with parents than is the case. This also means that a child joins a tutor group that can also nurture and protect. This has to be a smaller vertical tutor group that best resembles the idea of family. We should not throw children into the potential mayhem of thirty students all of the same age, hoping they will eventually find their best survival fit. This is potentially damaging to all parties and a high risk management strategy. The role of the tutor is as important as that of the parents and the part played by other students becomes supportive, important and lasting. The debate is not class size: it is tutor group size

4. Through trust and leadership opportunities to help others, the tutor grows self esteem and this is the real magic of learning. We return to those schools that see kids as powerful and *'active*

personality systems' and who understand the power of the supportive vertical pack, as opposed to the one that can turn on you and make your life hell. The tutor creates win/win situations and never ever leaves the child's side.

If we can get the start right, the child is best placed to complete the pyramidal journey to self esteem and beyond and this is what Vertical Tutoring seeks to do. The next stage of the journey is self-learning and the need to know. The teacher takes over from the tutor but the tutor never goes far. It is the only safe way of running a school and utilising positively the *'power of the pack'*. This ensures that young people become the leaders we need them to be by giving them the responsibilities and training we need them to have and they want to have. The secrets of the pyramid are the same as the secrets of the tutor. It is all about safety, self esteem and personal development, and the view that education requires a process and significant others to help.

Come Home VT

Magic Carpet

You have a magic carpet
That will whiz you through the air
To Maine or Spain or Africa
If you just tell it where,
So will you let it take you
Where you've never been before
Or will you buy some drapes to match
And use it on your floor?

Shel Silverstein

Chapter 11: Learning in the Front Office: Process Building

Boiling water takes a while for you to see any change, then all of a sudden things start to happen. Have faith in the process. We must know what changes to make.

W. Edwards Deming

History and the journey to VT

In one form or another VT has always been around. Arguably, the route to the 'modern' state version of Vertical Tutoring set out here began in the 1980s and involved a handful of schools that understood the need to manage variation better to maximise outcomes. Performance data was seen as a means of raising standards but also had the potential to measure organisational effectiveness and value for money. In those days they were the mavericks and knew only one thing; schools did not work properly and there had to be a better way and data held out many possibilities. As ever, there were too many people not working in schools telling those who did work in schools what to do, how to do it and trying to dictate direction. In those days, local authorities employed their own small army of County Inspectors and Advisers. Even then, the dependency on advisers was high and their demise allowed centralisation to become rampant.

It is interesting to note how long it takes in a system of centralist control for maverick innovation to become mainstream thinking. Back then, the challenge was how to use data software to maximise student outcomes and manage learning. It still is now for too many schools. From there, it was a small step to realise that parents and students held essential information needed to facilitate learning and guide practice. The answer was 'a deep learning conversation' or 'academic tutorial'; an annual meeting between the school, the parent and the child without time constraints. It is the case that data has always 'guided' teachers in schools but that alone is not sufficient to manage variation and predict learning outcomes. Schools have only a small part of the information needed and it is being information rich that explains the data and advises strategy and begins a process that builds a system. Information + data = knowledge.

It is all about building teams around learning rather than teaching. At present schools try to build back office support around the classroom almost completely by-passing parents, tutors and even students. Such arrangements appear to comply with the mantra that *'It is all about learning and teaching'* but this can result in hypercomplex structures whereby variation cannot be managed in an effective and affective way. This is especially so in schools organised in Year groups made rigid by the introduction of Key Stages. Year systems are obstacles to school improvement because they limit time with parents and restrict and undermine tutor capability in every way possible. There is no end to end learning process. Only governments would be foolish enough to bring in Curriculum style Key Stages and give the illusion that Year Systems connect learning and that Key Stage co-ordinators are somehow administratively and managerially important. Centralist intentions produce opposite outcomes: it is an organisational law. The whole purpose of management is to understand what variation is and manage it to improve and predict system outcomes, not pretend it isn't there and allow it to play havoc with detrimental effects.

Teaching subjects (target driven) and teaching children (learning driven) still continue to diverge rather than converge, especially as our school management behaviours and measures of success became increasingly attuned to targets, themselves driven by inspection. In the new ideology there is only teaching time and this is reinforced through the introduction of TLRs, which in the first phase failed to recognise any pastoral responsibilities for our apparently one dimensional charges. Consequently, the role of parents, tutors and tutees continues its long trend of neglect: beliefs and values over the last twenty years have been increasingly ignored or abandoned as time shrinks and the moral compass schools need no longer works.

Building a new model: VT

Missing from all of the SSAT models set out in the influential series 'A New Shape for Schooling?' (2006) is the conduit that creates an end-to-end operational system. We have a learning theory based on Hargreaves' idea of greater *'personalisation through co-construction'* that extols the virtues of relationships but places the teacher / student (classroom) relationship at the top. No mention is made of the importance of the tutor (assumed?) while the *'relationship with parents'* gets a three line mention as something to be resolved through the increased use of computers. Like the 'Deeps', any coherent learning process is simply missing and we are left with a jig-saw of ideas but no real picture to work from. The series of booklets produced by the SSAT is useful and provides an overview of good practice but breaks an important rule. Systems Thinking demands we cast a very critical eye over current practice and the powerful influences on that practice before presenting what schools do as best practice. The quest for a *'New Shape for Schooling'* is admirable and contains much of what is needed but requires an holistic approach; suggesting part solutions and strategies alone may mean that we end up embedding contradictions and persuading schools to copy bits of systems rather than entirely rethink their own.

The horizontal model does not work effectively on the ground and can now be dismissed. By placing a student at the heart of the school and recognising that parents and students hold missing information, things start to make more sense, including *'co-construction',* and we can start to build a Vertical Tutoring Culture within which the deconstructed 'Deeps' make more subservient sense.

Identifying the Key Players / Partners

In figure 10, the key players (significant others) in the learning life of the student are identified and recognised (a la Malaguzzi) and each contributes equally to learning success by providing information, support and partnership. However, this is not yet a management model because at this point relationships are assumed. To support the student requires focused attention from the tutor who accesses and draws down the immediate resources needed. This first model simply establishes and recognises the value of the key players closest to the student.

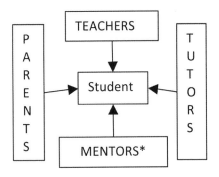

*Mentors are the immediate students in the tutor group. The most powerful of these learning relationships are tutor/student/ parents and tutor/student/mentor closely followed by teacher/ tutor/ student and teacher/student/mentor, but all combinations and others form and re-form as strategically needed. If this is the logical start to any operational learning process, building the rest of the organisation requires us to ask what a school is like as an organisation when these are put to the fore. In fact, what is happening is an expanded and more effective concept of co-construction: a way of developing learners and learning that involves all concerned parties in a self supporting way.

Without parents and a working co-construction model, variation cannot be enriched and managed. This is why very small schools win every time. What parents and teachers find in small schools is mutual partnership, recognition and validation (Carnie 2004:). In early years schools, children quite like their parents around but this all suddenly changes at secondary school. The component parts for organisational and individual success expressed by the very first schools to explore VT are

- ∞ **The academic tutorial involving tutor, tutee and parents (no time limit)**
- ∞ **Tracking and data systems**
- ∞ **Mixing older and younger students to support and role model learning**
- ∞ **Re-establishing the essential role of the tutor**
- ∞ **Returning to Houses as the key way of running the school**
- ∞ **Treating parents as equal partners in learning**

What dawned on the first vertically tutored schools is a harsh reality. Put simply, it is not possible to fully release the creativity of teachers and the potential of students without the partnership and support of families and without the local co-ordination of personal services. This is what customer services are and why it is helpful in describing schools using normal organisational terminology. Tutoring as the conduit for learning had been lost at some past point as an art and as a skill, and a key function of the school means returning tutoring to its rightful place where relationships form and work best. It was a cultural and organisational priority at the start of VT and remains so today.

To be effective and affective requires the means whereby parents, students and tutors can

- ∞ **Engage in a three-way discussion without time constraints (form partnerships)**
- ∞ **Collaborate on interpreting data and gathering information (academic tutorial)**
- ∞ **Agree learning strategies (support teaching and learning directly)**
- ∞ **Listen to each other's powerful stories about learning (consider the whole child)**
- ∞ **Draw down and use organisational services for personalised improvement (encourage innovation)**

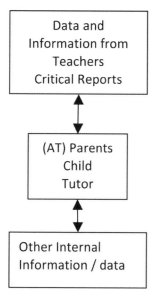

This provides an inclusive and values driven theory about learning beyond the assumed. It is nothing new but recognises that family ideals and input are fundamental to learning engagement. The child's immediate *'village'* comprises fellow tutees (mixed age), family and the tutor. Together, they redefine what it is to care and support: they value each other's contribution and develop each other's expertise. In management terms, these are all customers and teachers, each providing services, all managing variation and all delivering services. These are the basic learning concepts that determine how schools should operate as a joined up process.

Figure 11: The Deep Learning Conversation (Academic Tutorial): basic model

The key time in which the tutor, the family and the tutee engage is the AT (academic tutorial or *'deep learning conversation'*). This is an essential part of Vertical Tutoring and has several components: unlimited time (usually

35 minutes or so), a place to meet, all parties present, a full school report and other relevant data and an agreement to meet within a flexible time frame of one week. Information flows inwards to the AT from teachers and other internal and external agencies. The meeting is information rich and occurs at critical times in the learning life of the child. For Year 7 it should be within the first term and for Year 11 it should be immediately after mock examinations. Both are critical times for reflection, assessment and agreeing strategic planning and support. The tutor guides discussion. Flowing out from this are agreed learning strategies (up to three) that will be monitored formally and informally by the tutor and parents. This connects the four key players (parents, tutor, mentors and teachers) operationally and enhances the role of tutees as the focus of the learning process. This enables the school, for the first time, to provide front office services and build in value from the word go. It starts a school learning process and starts to establish the idea of a learning organisation.

The AT ensures that data and information is captured and that co-construction and variation become part of the strategic learning plan for each student. This also establishes part of the monitorial role of tutor time. Such partnership produces all kinds of insights, public and private, that enable the tutor to become highly effective and professional and build the kind of supportive relationships that extend into the classroom.

Attributes of Customers and Relationships

There are a host of relationships of various sorts active in schools at any one time. Unless these are rationalised, the organisation becomes hypercomplex and dysfunctional. Johnston and Clark (2001) helpfully describe these variables by citing various customer types. These are the parents that schools need to work with. All influence learning.

The Ally: willing to help out / respected by others. If this customer is happy, others will be too. This one may be on the PTA or be persuaded to become a governor by the smart Headteacher
The Hostage: locked into a certain view of how schools operate. Can be difficult if they feel the school is not performing properly and will not accept excuses
The Anarchist: dislikes rules; won't accept home/school partnership agreements. Their awkwardness persuades schools to be wary. Let the HOY handle this one
The Patient: very accepting of the school and similar to the hostage in accepting rules and regulations. However, too much restriction can turn the acquiescent into anarchists
The Tolerant: this is the person last to get served at the bar. It is unwise however to ignore them for long and 'it may be dangerous to trade on their apparent goodwill'
The Intolerant: these parents are always on the phone to the school. What started as a good relationship soon turned to one of stress, high demand and high maintenance. 'Without careful handling these people can easily turn into Terrorists'
The Victim: the parents attract misfortune. When some part of the system goes wrong, it is always their kid who is affected. They will then blow situations out of all proportion or simply be 'resigned to their inevitable fate'
The Terrorist: this parent mounts damaging attacks when you least expect it. This is the parent at a pleasant induction evening who will raise the school's *drug problem* from three years ago or plant something awful in the press after telling you the day before what a great school you have
The Incompetent: these parents are fairly clueless about how schools work, do not read letters home, miss appointments but need careful attention. Staff may find themselves threatened by these parents when the inevitable goes wrong again...
The Champion: all schools want champions who praise the school to the hilt, are supportive and who tell others how good the school is.

Of course, some may see that these also describe Headteachers but I couldn't possibly comment. The point is that schools should create allies out of customers and future champions. This requires a dialogue around their children far greater than schools allow. Only the tutor can do this because most require individualised customer care that prevents stereotyping and increases parental buy-in and effectiveness.

If these are the attributes of parent customers, the attributes of the service relationships require conceptualising. These have direct implications for the school's engagement with parents and the way partnership can be best achieved. Johnston and Clark (2001) suggest the following *key elements* marginally adapted here for schools

- ∞ **Communications:** the extent to which there is two-way communication; the ability to deliver clear messages, and the ability to listen.
- ∞ **Trust:** the degree to which one partner depends on the work or recommendations of the other without seeking extra justification or collaboration. In some cases the partner may commit the other to work without prior consultation.
- ∞ **Intimacy:** the extent to which information is shared for the benefit of removing barriers to learning through better support strategies.
- ∞ **Rules:** a mutual acceptance of how this particular relationship operates: what is acceptable and desirable and what is not.

All of the above combine to build a learning process and have operational implications around training, pay, roles, management, leadership etc. A school's relationship with customers requires considerably more attention than the assumptions schools rely upon.

Redesigning a school

It is not possible to make the two ideas (horizontal tutoring and deep conversations with parents and students) organisationally coherent without skimping and breaking learning as a process. This is currently a management and learning disaster reflected in bad ideas like review days, rolling academic tutorials, group approaches, kids being asked to set their own targets and other similar models still popular with most schools. To do this properly, a tutor has to listen to and engage with parents and the tutee. Each has an important story to tell about learning and each story is a source of information that can promote student learning and make the role of the tutor a professional one. The child learner is not a target driven entity but a whole child with emotions, pressures and challenges living in a difficult world driven by fear of failure, climate change and conflict.

The changes needed are largely unproblematic. Schools choose to see problems because it is their organisational nature to be driven by constraints rather than values. Tutor group size should never be above 18 (11-16) and many schools are capable of getting this number down further. It is a paradox that it is a vertical system that best supports a horizontal structure though the future will be entirely vertical for the 'star' school innovators! Moving to a vertical system involves a number of stages.

This means the return of very experienced staff to tutoring; it also means non-teaching staff taking on tutor roles and all of this is just the start. There are many challenges, but schools are often at their very best when they elect to leap into the stream of 'best bet chaos.' This has always been the quickest way to the future for risk-takers and those able to listen and understand the noise at the periphery. What Vertical Tutoring (VT) offers is a complete management makeover that ensures the release of creativity and innovation. It is entirely about relationships and how people work together to maximise potential and it is this which creates the values driven school.

Creating the mature VT school

1. The sizes of tutor groups has to decrease (maximum 18 students if possible)
2. The number of tutor groups equals the number of tutor spaces available in the school
3. The tutor groups needs to be reorganised and balanced (age, gender, ability)
4. Parents, students need to be consulted and governor support in place
5. ICT data systems have to do what they are intended to do to support cultural change and vertical groups
6. External training is needed to enable Systems Thinking and cultural change
7. Planning needs to be in place
8. The Head and Leadership Team need a deep understanding of VT and be up to the task and should be the first to be managerially trained in Systems Thinking

It is now possible to see the school as an Information Market where customers rule and where everyone understands their role in the learning process and each provides services.

Fig 12 (below) indicates the following in brief. It is not the final VT model but indicates that

1. Vertical tutor groups have been established and tutors allocated. The formation of tutor groups is not based on friendship but on creating balanced groups. Lead Tutors are chosen from the full staff list including NTS (Non Teaching Staff) and senior staff
2. Families and tutors liaise. Each is dependent on the other. This reduces anxiety and complaints (demands) and supports learning. It also begins to shape how the school should operate end to end
3. The tutor is the conduit and draws down services on behalf of the parent client for a tutee. This defines how resources are delivered and creates an internal service / customer market
4. Tutoring is primarily about supporting Learners and monitoring performance (building learning relationships).Tutee and tutor work together.

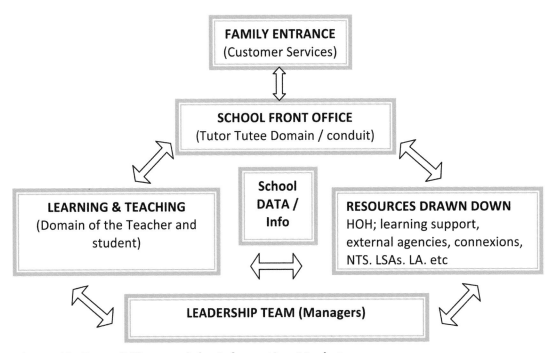

Figure 12: Front Offices and the Information Market

5. The HOH (Head of House) is now a School Leader and a resource. The Head of House is effectively the Head of a School and this is not the same as being a HOY (super secretary)

6. The role of the tutor is to ensure that tutees can engage with learning (build Learning Relationships). There is no time to deliver programmes but the tutor may deliver important topics preferably through older student leaders. Remember VT is SEAL and will be some of the best PSHE in the school (paradoxically) but programmes are not taught as such, though this may develop as vertical systems start to overtake and overhaul horizontal ones. This is tutor / tutee time.

7. All teachers / support staff are also tutors and this ensures that everyone understands every job and how things work (process). This flattens management and ensures that all involved understand the school system and their role in it. In turn, this enhances the possibility for greater innovation. This allows the management / leadership function to impact on the system process rather than people

8. The Leadership Team removes all barriers to learning and learning relationships and transforms management structures to suit

9. Everyone is a teacher, a leader and a learner (tutor, parent, tutee, teacher, LSAs)

10. Everyone supplies information and services, but tutoring is the key support and communications conduit and the focal point of the learning process.

In this way, families and learners are less likely to be lost in the complex back office of resource services. By having the tutor as conduit (mentor / advocate / facilitator), it means that the school can be remodelled to provide services more efficiently by greatly improving the management of variation. In this way quality is increasingly built into the process and driven by customer partnership and internal innovation. Teachers are much more likely to see more engaged students from a revamped tutorial system than from an inefficient pastoral system. In fact, the pastoral system (in the USA the counselling system: in France the monitoring system) has been upgraded and improved and no longer exists as it did; it has been largely replaced and determined by tutoring and by leadership. All teachers are also tutors (regardless of status) and work with tutors to resolve learning issues. The tutor accesses resources and especially the services of older students, all of whom are trained by the school to lead and support (citizenship), by building the idea of citizenship through trust and responsibility, raising esteem across the school. It is the job of tutors to prepare and support tutees prior to and during their classroom experience time.

In terms of assessment for learning and co-construction, the AT is a powerful driver of school improvement. At the front office conference table is a Full School Report and any additional data needed. This must include clear comments from staff which should include observations of any learning barriers, improvement strategies, attendance issues and test results. The richer the school's input the better the tutor and parent are able to support. This meeting (tutor, parents, tutee) brings together a full overview of learning, other factors (home) affecting performance and an identification of any support resources needed and strategies to be followed. The golden rule here is that while all data contains inaccuracies the real purpose of data is to raise questions: it is finding the answers to the questions that data raises which is important and this requires emotional and spiritual knowledge (human input from those closest i.e. parents and tutors: intimacy). The skill of the tutor is to prepare thoroughly, listen to others, ask inclusive questions, value the teaching role of parents and help identify up to three learning strategies that all can agree to. In this way the tutor's front office resembles a consultancy service where ownership of improvement strategies is shared and resources accessed. **The secret is to share ownership of learning with parents and students and to realise that the teacher is a main customer of the tutor.**

Redefining Parent Partnership

The tutor role redefines what people do in the school. It also redefines parent partnership by ensuring that the front office function is the catalyst for learning that unites home and school and so defines the system (*'shape'*) of the school. It does this by recognising for the first time what schools claim to believe; that parents are important and significant players in their child's learning. By providing a genuine partnership with the family, the tutor can perform three important tasks in a society fragmented by broken systems.

1. The tutor can support parents by building trust, valuing what they have to say and by keeping them informed (communications). Help parents be parents
2. The tutor can advise on learning strategies (teaching and learning) and draw down resource solutions from the wider school and from within the tutor group (support tutees)
3. The tutor can help to heal rifts and circumvent any difficulties so that parents feel supported and less isolated (healing and partnership)

NB. Headteachers and Leadership Teams can make errors of judgement, especially where VT is concerned. They do this by compromising and cherry picking. For example, they decide not to involve parents in AIs or place time limits on ATs. Some may decide not to involve the 6th Form or to exclude Year 7. These tend to be schools that often perform well as opposed to those that have struggled in the past. Either they do not understand VT (untrained and uninformed... ignorant and arrogant) or they are not values driven and diminish potential and opportunity. These schools reinvent old culture and abhor risk. I have seen schools do the oddest things in the name of VT mainly because they cannot let go of old culture or have not submitted to basic Systems Thinking. Any deviation from Systems Thinking and the values it supports means that what is being practised is VT in name only and that any coherent learning process has been diminished. The school has not transformed because leadership has chosen not to engage with a deep understanding of VT and its values.

Chapter 12: Building an Upside Down School

Back to the Deeps, Learning Gateways and VT

What the Upside Down School Model does (fig. 13) is show in a very precise way how the nine gateways actually link and how each can be differentially accessed. This enables the four 'deeps' to be organisationally resolved by following a Systems Thinking approach and applying sound management principles as exercised in mature vertically tutored schools. The model is one of customer relations, information flow and process. Executed with care, Vertical Tutoring is cultural transformation. Everything changes over time but is felt immediately from day one. We now have the possibility of every person in and beyond the school doing the right job after decades of being tied by centralist red tape and driven by obscure targets to perform the wrong jobs. **The semantics of student voice, collaboration, partnership, co-construction, assessment for learning and 'care' itself are overtly redefined by VT and this is just the beginning.**

We can ensure in this more sophisticated but simpler model that good data and information underpin the strengths and professionalism of all key players but especially the tutor's ability to be the mentor / advocate. This enables the tutor to provide

- (a) Pastoral and academic guidance
- (b) High quality parent partnership
- (c) Mentoring support and leadership from other students

...in fact, precisely what it says in the tutor's job description set out previously.

Within the vertical tutor group, a given student has a range of mentoring and leadership opportunities available to him/her adding hugely to the effectiveness of the organisation and the opportunity for students to be Good Samaritans and good learners. The power of the vertical pack becomes a positive force rather than one of risk.

In effect, the school is able to build on a range of 'learning relationships' and this increases efficiency, a sense of joint purpose and fun. Instead of separating out and isolating areas such as pastoral and academic, they are united through the tutor and the front office. All of this greatly enhances communications, working relationships and achievement and should define what management and leadership is needed. This also makes possible the idea that every child actually does matter because it is now possible to demonstrate 'deeply' what it is to care, nurture and build esteem and so better enable learning. In effect, the school is living a 'deep' theory of learning.

The tutor becomes personal and powerful and has made the shift from being *'the sage on the stage'* to *'the guide by the side'*. The parent is granted full access rights to their own child's learning, so often denied them. The teacher is better supported by significant others and especially by top quality, rejuvenated tutoring of which they are part. Student voice has made the transition from councils to active citizenship and leadership. We can even make sense of Citizenship. This was only ever part of a subject: it is active citizenship that is important and this is all about how we run our schools.

At the same time the role of the Leadership Team is clear. It is fundamentally to make the lives of all personnel effective and fun and this means identifying and removing all current barriers to learning. It is to build organisations and grow people that have the capacity and wit to learn. This, essentially, is what a creative learning organisation populated with highly creative people, does. It does this by ensuring that human relationships are de rigueur and as such need time: it ensures listening (skills) and it allows for the development of the full range of amazing human attributes that our teachers possess but which are too often organisationally denied. It recognises that the person doing the job is the right person to do the job.

Similarly, schools claim to believe in CPD for their staff but again the concept is narrowly focused. Good organisations largely self train but always get in expertise when looking at systems. Yet, it is possible for teachers to live out their lives in an 11-18 school without ever knowing what a UCAS form is or ever having the opportunity to engage with sixth form students! Vertical tutoring opens up new possibilities for everyone to develop and to learn and this strengthens the school as an organisation by increasing the organisational knowledge base, developing staff and putting joy back into work.

It is only by listening to the stories of parents and students that a Headteacher can properly consider curriculum development. S/he soon realises that National Strategies need to be individual, human scale strategies and that real school improvement and curriculum development depends upon this. It is the richness of these tales from parents, staff and tutors that provides the information that informs the data that raises the questions that initiates new thinking. These are the conversations that creative people have and our teachers are hugely creative.

Learning Relationships

This phrase has been used throughout but has not been fully explained. Schools work hard on teaching and learning, the classroom learning relationship shared by teacher and student. However, this cannot work in isolation from other relationships within a school and school systems need to promote other valid learning relationships because of their interconnectivity and capacity to promote co-construction. The tutor acting in an advisory and advocate role with the tutee is a learning relationship and a very critical one at that but to really work effectively often requires drawing in teachers, parents and the power of the tutor group.

It is these triple whammy relationships that are made highly effective in VT because they build in the high quality support and services that prevent mistakes by focusing unswervingly on customer care.
The following are the main examples because they are tutor facilitated and tutee focused:-

- ∞ Tutor, tutee, parent
- ∞ Tutor, tutee, teacher,
- ∞ Tutor, tutee, mentor
- ∞ Tutor, tutee, support staff
- ∞ Potentially, parent, tutee, mentor

At this point, we have to remember that building in quality costs nothing. We are removing from a system of considerable stress and waste and giving back time to do more interesting and relevant learning support tasks. How this is done requires further Systems Thinking and requires staff training but it is not a difficult task. What is difficult is the unlearning and deprogramming of leadership teams and the process of changing hearts and minds (Systems Thinking). Most front line teachers and tutors understand the values of VT immediately because it is common sense and it is this that has been removed from our schools by quasi, pseudo scientific approaches to schooling that are centrally driven.

It is within the process of building and underpinning a variety of effective support relationships that quality can be built into the operational structure. These are the drivers of school improvement that schools should develop beyond 'belief' because they will best secure improved learning outcomes. They will also provide tremendous scope for innovation: the territory is largely unexplored.

Just as the former Head of Year has moved from being a super secretary and counsellor to a Leader of a House (ostensibly Head of a small school) so the tutor has moved from being admin/PSHE to being the Head of a small school (the tutor group).

Information Markets / Service markets / Learning contracts

If we now look closely at schools, it is possible to see how they might work better and how the process parts work together.

Information market

Information on every child is now focused in the right place, with the tutor, next to the child and within reach of (and partnership with) parents (Front Office). The tutor controls the information and communications flow in and out and draws down any resources needed, besides providing other mentoring and leadership support from within the immediate tutor group. In this way, the tutor interprets information and secures the best strategies to progress and to support learning. This reduces complaint demands (system waste) and redefines how back office systems should function and the tasks that need to be performed by support staff. (These are also tutors.) The Tutor is a customer of the

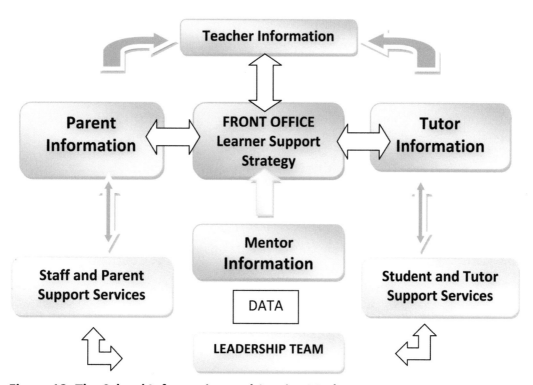

Figure 13: The School Information and Service Market

school and also a supplier; the school provides the means (time, information, support) for the tutor to be an effective tutor and build the learning process from this point. In other words, the school treats the tutor as a customer to ensure that the tutor has what is needed to be effective. In the same way, teachers are customers of tutors who provide teachers with support services such as monitoring overall performance, home liaison, learning support, guidance and planned, negotiated intervention. By doing this the teacher becomes a more effective teacher. This is the start of the process that enables the teacher to teach even better; this is because the learner will be ready to engage with learning, ensuring that the learner is not returned to the repair shop as *damaged goods*. By establishing the tutor as a conduit, less information is lost in the backroom to the great benefit of the more vulnerable children and to learners in general.

The school's back office is there to support the tutor first (school's front office) because of the tutor's conduit 'need to know' role with parents and staff. Students too are leaders, service providers and customers enabling learning capability and self-esteem to grow.

Tutors and internal markets

The Vertical Tutoring Models pose different management challenges. The key challenge to the school's Leadership Team (LT) is to answer three questions:

1. **How can the LT release the huge creativity inherent in teachers, tutors, support staff, students and parents to raise achievement and improve outcomes?**
2. **How can the LT inspire and give time to building these critical Learning Relationships so that all are engaged in a shared ownership of learning?**
3. **How can the LT transform the management structure to facilitate VT and answer Q1 and Q2?**

To answer these questions there has to be a shared organisational understanding that the *'core'* business (teaching and learning) and the *'care'* business (academic and pastoral support for learning) need to be a single process on the learning continuum. Together they form a view of the *'whole child'* which is critical if learning is to be properly supported by the school community and especially the tutor group.

Any answers from the LT involve the following

- ∞ A small time investment for tutor time (20-25 minutes at least 4/5 times)
- ∞ Moving tutor time. This must not be at the start of the day, at the end of the day and not straight after lunch. The session before break is ideal.
- ∞ Establishing open-ended ATs at critical learning times to enable deep learning conversations that must include parents / carers.

It is this internal information market (above and below) of stakeholder voices that is the main driver of system change and of school improvement. In essence, this is the way a mature vertically tutored school ensures high quality customer care, is able to predict future needs and secure better learning outcomes. **This market of voices, stories, feedback, and support is the rich canvas of creative chaos that not only builds the emotional platforms of confidence and improved self-esteem but enables learners to take the next steps with their teachers. It is also the blueprint for the design of school management and even school architecture!**

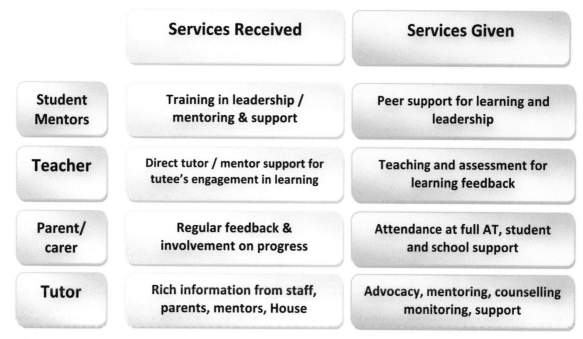

	Services Received	Services Given
Student Mentors	Training in leadership / mentoring & support	Peer support for learning and leadership
Teacher	Direct tutor / mentor support for tutee's engagement in learning	Teaching and assessment for learning feedback
Parent/ carer	Regular feedback & involvement on progress	Attendance at full AT, student and school support
Tutor	Rich information from staff, parents, mentors, House	Advocacy, mentoring, counselling monitoring, support

Figure 14: Service Agreements within the Information Market

A brief explanation and analysis of the above is as follows

a) All tutees (Year 10 is good) at some point will receive high quality training and support in leadership and mentoring by the school. Some will opt for extra training to deliver learning programmes such as phonetic reading schemes. Some will be asked to support subject areas or even aspects of behaviour management, all under the guidance of the form tutor. These might seem strange but all of these are happening to at least a small extent in most schools already. However, instead of being bolt-on and ad hoc, all students are involved. Every student, not the few, will have the opportunity to demonstrate leadership and accept responsibility and be trusted. **Older students will all be Co-Tutors.** This changes rewards systems, CPD and even the school management structure. Every student is surrounded by a bespoke learning support network facilitated by the form tutor that seeks to improve learning access through the provision of constant, needs based support, advocacy and parent partnership.

b) Tutors will have already pre-prepared tutees for the classroom. However, teachers can expect the tutor to respond to classroom learning and support needs by accessing the power of the tutor group pack, home contact or direct tutor intervention to support classroom learning. Teachers will also have their own departmental support. Teachers will always go direct to the tutor and not to the HOH (Head of House). The tutor will go to the HOH (Headteacher of the House) as needed for extra support and advice. In short, the tutor receives information from the teacher and decides how to best support the learner. This is a highly creative and personal service which is what tutoring was always meant to be and maintains a direct home link while defining back room management behaviour. As success increases, negative work demands decrease.

c) Parents can expect to have direct communications with the tutor who in turn keeps the parent / carer briefed and informed of progress on a needs basis. At least once a year there will be a full academic tutorial (about 45 minutes) to review learning, agree tutee-centred learning strategies and share information using a full written report and other assessment data. This meeting and relevant full report takes place at critical learning times, and not necessarily at the end of a year or at the beginning! In turn, parents will be more encouraged to support the school in every way they can because they feel valued and better informed. Such a system does not overpower the tutor but actually reduces demand complaints and makes the school work properly.

d) The tutor is thus supplied with essential pastoral and assessment information from teachers, support staff, parents and any mentors that are peculiar to tutees. This information is used to underpin learning and provide leadership opportunities that raise self-esteem, increase confidence and improve engagement with learning. The tutor ensures that home and school maintain a dialogue so that values and strategies around learning are shared.

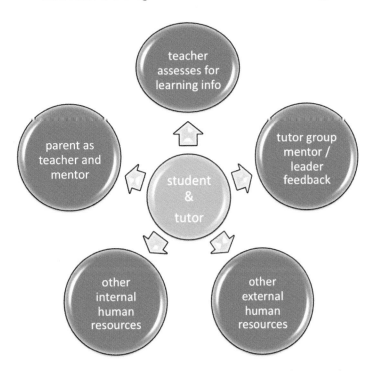

e) The tutee receives pre-emptive feedback and access to a variety of non-classroom tutor based support from peers, mentors, or via external agencies; the tutor is at the hub deciding the best options with other school experts. The tutee knows that the tutor will always be there to guide and to support and be the stalwart advocate in difficult times. The tutor will never leave the tutee's side until they grow into the leader citizens we need.

Figure 15: Drawing Down Resources

f) The school management system *transforms* to ensure that the information and support market works, develops and innovates to provide ever higher quality services. In particular, the school ensures that the tutor is surrounded by trained tutees in a balanced tutor group, external expertise and excellent House Leadership.

The tutor and the student are now the centre of the school's learning universe. Other internal resources needed by the tutor include the SENCO, support staff and Head of House. External support includes Connexions, employers, other LA services etc. Reducing the bureaucracy and increasing the efficiency of how this is done requires innovative thinking; current methodology is too bureaucratic. The tutor facilitates (draws down and applies) what services are needed from the five feeder circles (above). The parent accesses services via the tutor who actions whatever is needed. Everyone is a teacher, everyone a learner, everyone a customer, everyone a service provider, everyone a beneficiary.

By having a concept of a front office as the domain of the tutor group where family and school meet, the management of the school is clearer. It is there to facilitate the flow of resources and information around the student learner via the tutor (effective and fun). The fun or *'joy in work'* comes from success and job fulfilment. This is how school improvement works. First, we take apart and examine the system that exists, then tidy up the system and remove all Year based barriers. Once this has been done, it is a question of the degree to which the school can walk the talk of values and moral purpose.

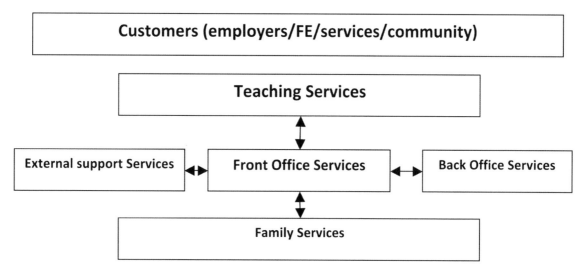

Figure 16: Customer Services and Communications

This is not what we have now. Schools are working heroically at trying to make poor systems and practices work and there are real doubts as to whether Heads can fully grasp what needs to be done to properly transfer to a vertical culture. What is clear is that the key people who need to understand VT at a deep level are those in the Leadership Team. It needs to be understood that building in quality and excellence through enhanced learning relationships requires a complete system overhaul, but over time. The school as a system changes and evolves in phases as new system demands arise. It is evolution not revolution, but evolution in a term and then every day. The Head may well ask how to approach such a task given his / her circumstances: W. Edwards Deming would say, *'You're the manager, you figure it out!'* The other answer is to walk the talk of values and Systems Thinking.

Any new approach places the Tutor and the Tutor Group at the heart of the school but not in its bad old form. It is in and around the tutor group that the key learning relationships are formed and it is the tutor who has the principal responsibility to nurture and develop these in new and exciting ways. This is Hargreaves' Deep Model in practice. In his pamphlet, Hargreaves quotes Sizer (1984). *'The key worker in a school is the student. The only important product is his or her learning. All else is a matter of means'.* This is true, but needs to be understood. Sizer places the teacher within the 'means' together with all other players, tutors, family, peers and teachers. All must support learning and not prop up failing factory style systems that cannot be made to work effectively or which fall short of a relevant and coherent contribution to learning. Sadly, when most schools introduce VT, the organisation of the school day comes well before the organisation of learning. The latter has to 'fit round' the former and this makes management teams and the school 'value less' and always diminishes.

This may sound at first to be a massive task for the tutor requiring extra time, but this is not so. In fact, tutors in mature (trained) VT schools are less stressed, more fulfilled and more effective and so is everyone else.

In his later years, Maslow talked about *'one world'* with no nations. He said that's the way it must be except no-one knows it yet. Vertical Tutoring is similar. Everybody should win: unless of course Leadership Teams mess it up, and that is what many do: it is not their fault. Centralism truly messes with your *Head*. The motto of too many Leadership Teams is, *'We already do that'.* They don't of course, but they can't see it and won't accept advice. This is not just about thinking outside of the centralist box but is a) first realising that you are in a box and b) that getting a

warped sense of job fulfilment and enjoyment from life in a well ordered box is not going to improve anything.

The Front Office Partnership Contract

Above, note was made of the need for all to understand the system and how it works. This requires rules. Secondary education schools are a customer of Primary education schools. If the primary schools fail to deliver, the secondary school has to work harder on the *repair side* than it should and resources are wasted because complaint demands increase. This applies to parents. **Parents have a moral duty to supply services and this should be a legally supported set of obligations.** Everyone in this system gets paid by the state. The services that parents supply should ensure that children arrive at school on time, able to behave and able to read English to their chronological age (or at least well on the road to literacy). This should be supported by *early years* partnership, health workers and others and, when necessary, parents held to account. Of all the abuses that government is paranoid about, the most important is learning abuse. This is one children rarely recover from. World class education, western style, relies on a system that works and where all play their part. Government needs to supply services at the base of the system where maximal intervention is necessary and get their backsides out of the system where their prescription, bureaucracy and regulation gets in everyone's way.

Chapter 13: VT. And Organisational Change

Long-term commitment to new learning and new philosophy is required of any management that seeks transformation. The timid and the fainthearted, and the people that expect quick results, are doomed to disappointment.

W. Edwards Deming

Focusing on Transformation

In this chapter we need to return to the school and map out some of the changes, challenges and dangers in and around Vertical Tutoring. This is not a step by step guide, but an attempt to clarify signposts along the way and some of the guidelines needed.

The above models have managerial implications and require real leadership as opposed to the confusion of compliance, education and tick boxes that have ridden roughshod over values. The following table began with Kanter (1989) and was adapted by Barnard (2000) in *'Chaos, Culture and Third Millennium Schools'.*

Table 8: Bureaucracies v Post Entrepreneurial Organisations: adapted from Kanter, R. (1989)

Bureaucracies (horizontal system of schooling)	Post entrepreneurial (Vertical tutoring)
Bureaucratic	Post Entrepreneurial
Position Centred	Person and Process centred
Repetition Oriented	Creation Oriented
Rules Oriented	Outcomes and learning Oriented
Paid for Status	Paid for Contribution
Formal Channels	Expanded Access to Communications / resources
Assigned Territories	Cross Pollination via Front Office
Seek Ownership	Seek Experimentation / Innovation

Belbin (1996) described bureaucracy as '...*doing things right rather than doing the right thing'*. The switch to VT ensures that work works and that everybody can now do the right thing in a better way. There can be little doubt that schools are bureaucracies and need to understand how to move to a more focused and more flexible (tight and loose) system. These descriptors are the signposts that tell schools where they are and what the organisation should look and feel like on the journey to transformation.

To make the transition from one kind of organisational culture to another means changing what people do and identifying what drives people, their work and the support they need.

As Indicated (below) Kanter's descriptors can be broken down further and applied to facets of the school, in this case tutoring. The move to VT is a process of re-engineering but the key markers, set out below, will be almost immediate (day one of VT) if the preparation is sound, values and principles (appendix 1) adhered to and staff trained, prepared and involved. On day one, the key learning relationships will have already been established before the tutor group meets all together. This is done by carefully preparing tutors and tutees in a manner that allows sound learning relationships to form. Suffice it to say, this is where experienced advice and training is required. Change is always a journey but the beautiful thing about Vertical Tutoring is its simplicity. The signposts for the journey are values and clear management principles. If we value relationships we need to be very clear how to build in the trust needed.

Adding Value / Building in Value

The phrase 'added value' is helpful in one sense but misleading in another. Good organisations build value in so that it lasts and applies across the board: once value is built-in (and not until) it may then be possible to add value. Each is dependent on the other to a degree. The important thing is to continually improve the service by acting on the process. Adding something on can separate the process from the outcome and misinterpret the management role. There are four key places where value can be considerably built-in by a secondary school.

- ∞ Investing staff and expertise into feeder schools, including joint training (Trust School Model)
- ∞ The tutor / parent / child interface
- ∞ The tutor / tutee / mentor trinity
- ∞ The tutor / teacher / tutee trinity

Later, we can add the classroom (teacher / student) as another quality and improvement area but this is dependent on the previous time investments working properly as a process.

The chart (below) illustrates some of the key changes. In vertical systems, everyone (both teaching staff and support staff) has the potential to be a world class tutor because the learning process starts with them and builds from this base by establishing high quality support and learning relationships.

Table 9: Horizontal v. Vertical Organisational Characteristics

Horizontal	Vertical
Low Mentoring Opportunities	**High Mentoring/leadership Opportunities**
Lower Order Tutor Skills	**Higher Order Tutor Skills**
Variable Student / Tutor Attention	**Focused Attention by Need**
Behaviour Dominated	**Collaboration / Learning Dominated**
High Stress and High Control	**Low Stress and Shared Control**
Leadership Opportunities for the Few	**Leadership Opportunities for All**
Year Ethos Difficulties	**House Ethos Opportunities**
Tutor Isolated by Year	**Tutor Integrated by House**
Head of Year Isolated by Role	**HOH Team Runs the School(s)**
No Effective Academic Tutorial	**Effective Deep Learning Tutorial**
Weak Parental Partnership	**Strong Parental Engagement**
Tutors Often seen as Low Status Staff	**Tutors High Status**
Big Tutor Groups: Few Tutors	**Small Groups: Almost Everyone a Tutor**

More guidance is needed. Set out below are some of the basic rules or principles that schools should follow: not consider, not adapt. A bit of prescription won't hurt! Schools should follow these because they are values driven and managerially innovative and sound. If they are not followed, VT will be diminished and this will impact negatively on children and their engagement with learning as a process.

Set out here is a small starter selection of Golden Rules for successful VT.

1. **The number of rooms (all rooms) in a school equals the number of tutor groups**
2. **Tutor group size must be as low as possible and rarely above 20 in 11-16 schools. Where this is not possible add a second (assistant) tutor**
3. **Nobody is allowed to join the school as a teaching or support assistant without the idea that they will become a tutor or assistant tutor**
4. **All staff should be properly prepared and trained. Copying the local school is uncreative, rarely works and may spread bad practice**
5. **Tutor time is about 25 minutes and should ideally occur just before morning break**
6. **All staff are attached to tutor groups and to Houses / Colleges / Communities**
7. **Tutor Groups are not chosen on a friendship basis but on balanced grouping**
8. **All older students are trained in Leadership and Mentoring to be co-tutors**
9. **Almost all staff should be tutors**
10. **Heads of House should work from the same area, not separate offices**

The reasons why the Golden Rules and Principles of VT (see appendix) are important and need to be followed wherever possible (ref. 1-8 above) are as follows. There are many others...

Ref.1 and 2 above

Central to successful implementation of VT is the size of the tutor group. This is because at the heart of VT are learning relationships and especially that of the Tutor and Tutee. In particular, experience suggests that there should never be more than four students from a given year group. The way tutees are involved and supported by the tutor and supported by the school prior to VT is critical and there appears to be an optimal level bound by tutor group year size, not just verticality. This is all about group dynamics and optimum levels of learning relationship management

Ref. 3 and 6 above

Once the number of tutor groups is established, the number of tutors needed increases. Tutors are chosen from the complete staff list regardless of status. Most teachers will be tutors and most support staff involved either as Lead Tutors or Assistant Tutors. That means that all staff joining the school to work with children also become tutors and will be trained accordingly. Everyone must understand that to be effective all employees must know how the front office works and how systems support responds (process). Everyone a tutor.

Ref. 4 above

By copying the local school, there is a high chance of copying mistakes and trying to cherry-pick. Bolting bits on to inadequate systems never works. Without training, how can schools know what to ask and what to look for? VT is a major cultural change and not to be taken lightly. Systems Thinking requires management expertise. Training the tutors is the easy bit.

Ref. 5 above

Tutor time moves because there is an optimum time and place for tutoring. Anywhere else and the tutor is undermined and devalued. The *'It's only tutor time'*, syndrome.

Ref. 7 above

When tutor groups are formed we must think of the *'Dog Whisperer'* or in this case *'the school whisperer'*. The idea is to form a balanced pack and balanced Houses. Friendship is unimportant except in very unusual situations and can damage the balance needed.

Ref. 8 above

Training students is as important as training staff. Often there should be joint training!

There is so much more to tell but this is the start. VT needs to retain some of its mystery! Unless there is transformational system change, Vertical Tutoring will not release the powerful forces of creativity a school needs so that all can learn effectively and contribute equally. There are many other Golden Rules but I mustn't be overly prescriptive and schools that think will discover them and add to them as they go!

'We already do that' and 'We have made the decision...'

At the very heart of our schools is a massive problem. It is the damage done to school leadership by centralism and poor training. It is the reason why schools are not able to easily shift from factory thinking to transformational thinking: in effect, from an emphasis on teaching systems to an emphasis on learning systems (Ch. 1). It is not the fault of school leaders. Most school leadership teams are outstanding and hugely caring of their staff and understandably wary of change. Change is sometimes seen as disruptive, negative and a sign of weak management (a change of mind or admitting a past error in a system intolerant of mistakes) rather than a positive change of culture which is exciting, safe and fun.

Vertical Tutoring is a learning journey from where we are through the foothills of emotional intelligence and forward to higher, spiritual intelligence. The values set out in all school prospectuses are the same as those underpinning VT. The difference is in delivery and means. Vertical Tutoring is a values driven culture, not a target driven culture: VT will, however, ensure that 'targets' will be achieved faster and safer and with greater fun than any other system because it re-engineers schools around the real partnership strengths of parents, co-construction and the amazingly talented people who walk our school corridors every day. VT builds permanent and lasting learning relationships and cherishes them and does not tolerate barriers that get in the way of good people trying to do a good job. Schools really are blessed and so are we to have them.

When, in my passion for VT, I point out mistakes and compromises, these are not criticisms of schools but of what has caused schools to make such compromises. What Heads do is always done in what Heads consider to be the best interests of the school. As I always say, what makes leadership teams and all school staff so breathtakingly good is their ability to get the best out of a western system that is so compromised, badly constructed and potentially damaging that they can actually make it seem to work and even, on occasion, spark into unexpected life.

The Frank Sinatra syndrome (We did it our way)

Schools feel compelled to compromise values because the school as an organisation is geared round classroom teaching, Diplomas (pupils all over the place), break times, lunch arrangements, timetables, seemingly endless rules and regulations, staffing contracts and various reforms and quasi agreements that not only do not *reform* but are not of the school's making. This is before schools hit strange, restrictive practices, endless regulation and more besides. Learning is always built around school systems rather than being the system. In VT the school day and all else are potential barriers to the learning relationships that nurture engagement with learning. It is the function of LTs to see these things as blockages to be removed as imposters pretending to be more important than they are.

We also need to bear in mind that stress costs UK employers £38b every year and that teaching is a very stressful job. It costs in every way. Reducing stress is important.

Whenever a school goes vertical and says the fateful words, *'We'll do it our way'* or *'We have already made the decision* (before taking any real advice and training) *to …'*, I know then that the damage of ignorance and arrogance has already set in. It is usually an insecure Deputy Head who is running the school or a headteacher blinded by limitations. Both phrases ring the loud alarm bells of compromise. When we compromise values we always diminish the human spirit. When we compromise learning, we can damage the life chances of young people forever. In fact, schools that *'implement VT',* rarely implement VT. VT is a culture to be adopted: everything changes over time.

Compromising Values

Briefly set out here are a few of the many ways in which schools compromise values viewed from both a Systems Thinking and educational perspective.

1. We cannot move T/T (tutor time) from the start of the day

Schools can but sometimes don't because of *'important logistical reasons'* like lunch arrangements and a timetable frozen by the complexity of Diplomas. This means that what should be valued highly is compromised. Instead of valuing the tutor and T/T by moving T/T to a better slot (ideally before morning break) tutors are asked to perform their magic at a time when registration, admin and petty rules collide undermining the tutor and the learning relationships needed. (**Causes**: lack of will to acknowledge and remove barriers: lack of knowledge and belief regarding VT and its management: allowing logistical arrangements to have precedence over values and learning: not understanding Systems Thinking)

2. We don't want to involve Y7 in Vertical Tutoring

Schools tend to give two reasons for this: The first an overprotective view of Year 7. Year 7 is seen as *'precious'* and *'not ready'* for full induction. They need extra *'care'.* This usually means that the school is unwilling to upset the Y7 liaison person or erroneously thinks older students are a bad influence when the opposite is the case. Y7 are the main beneficiaries of VT. The second involves a perceived opportunity to provide an *'accelerated learning to learn programme'* that is tutor based. This is all about achieving future targets. Schools see this as a need to compensate for earlier systems failure. This is old culture thinking. Again, this undermines tutoring and students by making the year Y8-Y11 tutor group unbalanced and is full of assumptions about how students best progress and engage with learning.

(**Causes**: old culture Systems Thinking: compliance posing as innovation: insecure LT and inability to transform: lack of will to remove barriers and a lack of knowledge about VT)

3. Tutors should also teach PSHE/Citizenship/SEAL

Many schools, thankfully, have abandoned the idea that tutors should teach PSHE/citizenship. Some persist and see tutor time as a space to be filled or they give tutors an hour of timetable time to deliver PSHE type programmes (currently being made a legal obligation by foolish politicians). The idea that PSHE and tutor/learning relationships are easily connected is deeply flawed and misunderstands how learning relationships form. Schools sometimes want to get tutors to teach a SEAL programme in tutor time. Apparently this enables them to get a *Healthy Schools' Certificate*. VT is SEAL and VT is healthy schools. Healthy Schools certificates, ArtsMark Awards, Investors in People all absorb time and for what? Why not spend that time transforming: the school will be healthier, learning will improve and IiP will be made redundant? (**Cause**: old cultural ideas and assumptions: Ideology before common sense and not listening to staff and students: no philosophy of or theory of learning relationships: no theory of learning and no belief in the power of the pack and the tutor: assumptions everywhere)

4. Tutor group size too big

Many schools make no change to the size of tutor groups. This exponentially adds difficulty to the tutor task of forming high quality learning relationship, and establishing efficient drawdown of resources. It also undermines any concept of a front office, causing communications to be more problematic not less. The fundamental reason for tutor group size has been ignored and assumed. Tutor groups should never contain more than four students from a single year group: there are important group dynamics involved that have to be considered. (**Cause**: training failure: old culture thinking and high system *arrogance and ignorance*, weak management [tutors chosen from volunteers rather than from the complete staff list including support staff]: no learning theory: willingness to compromise values in favour of structures that cannot work).

The cause of these kinds of compromises and poor practices have been set out and anticipated by Deming: poor grasp of people psychology and emotional intelligence; low management knowledge base about variation; no appreciation of Systems Thinking and no working theory of knowledge.

These are not the fault of Headteachers: it is the damage of centralisation and an NPQH that cannot find a way to walk the talk of its own philosophy and *'open minds'*, a SSAT that shares around practices that invite cherry-picking and so legitimise old culture, an Innovation Unit that wouldn't know an innovation from recycled waste, and an examination system that changes like the sands to suit whatever political wind is blowing and...

When schools combine some of the system faults (above), the values of VT are greatly diminished to the point where schools are not really VT at all. It is just a superficial pretence. Outcomes are put at risk and tutor stress rises. Sadly, such schools pass their high risk strategies to others like a contagion, believing that their practice is good practice. This process is made worse by trainers who think they understand VT and its management but don't. They should know better but they don't know better; our schools churn in old ruts and have come to value a sense of movement rather than a sense of change and destiny. We are not blunt enough with each other. SIP (school improvement partners) offer only minimal help and are more likely to underpin old culture than change it. Good people, constantly battling with a culture of endless regulation and powerful compliance.

Time to lighten up with a bit of homo ludens...

Let's play 'Vertical Tutor Tick Box'

This is for all readers (especially form tutors) who get this far. Schools that have gone VT know the SEF rules. Tick the box if the statement is true.

Question	True (√)	false (x)
1 Tutor group size has not changed significantly		
2 Tutors 'teach' SEAL/PSHE via 'packs' centrally drafted		
3 Tutor time is at the start of the day or the end or both		
4 Year 7 is excluded from your tutor group		
5 There are more than 4 tutees from any one Year in your T/G		
6 Little in the way of training/familiarisation was given re VT		
7 The students kicked up a fuss and/or went on strike about VT		
8 You work harder now that VT has been introduced		
9 You met your new vertical tutor group virtually all at once		
10 You do not have an Assistant Tutor to support your group		
11 None of the LT are vertical tutors, not even from the start		
13 Academic tutorials still have time limitations parents		
14 Academic tutorials do not involve parents		
15 The Leadership Team was not trained in VT Systems Thinking		
16 The school plans to introduce SEAL through tutors		

These statements are some of the basic ones. If many of the ticks are in the 'True' column, the school's change to VT was superficial and values and principles have been sacrificed for logistical reasons such as lunch arrangements or similar. Several ticks means there has been no transformation and the school will never accrue the full benefits of VT and neither will the students and parents. The more ticks in the yes column, the more distant the school is from Vertical Tutoring and the more it fails to support learning and tutors, and the school LT may have made things worse. Such a school is not values driven and still thinks in old cultural ways, believing that improvement is all about targets and that teachers have to be protected from change, when really they need protection from the Leadership Team which itself needs protection from centralist dogma. And that's the problem, not the challenge!

In many ways, tutor time is the simplest part of VT and, paradoxically, the easiest to get wrong.
Tutor time belongs to the tutor group and has to be seen as such. It is there for a specific set of reasons concerned with the partnership, preparation and support of learning. The tendency for school managers is to see tutor time as time that must be filled with the teaching of some sort of programmes. In this way, VT is seen as a remedy for a broken process: in other words, having made the structural alterations (reduced group size, double tutors, students as citizens etc) and then followed the transformation through, schools choose to believe that programmes come before relationships and veer off into old culture. The feedback from PGCE students and tutors nationwide tells a story of the bad ways in which VT has been implemented by LTs.

By having two tutors (Lead and Assistant) in the group and older students trained in leadership and teaching programmes (especially phonetic reading schemes) the tutor is surrounded by human resources.

This makes the nature of vertical tutor time very different to most current systems. In essence, if not totality, **student voice is tutor time** when old and young join to discuss bullying policy or whatever is

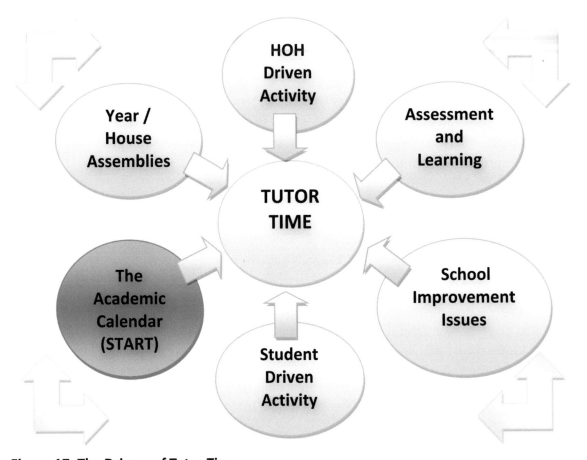

Figure 17: The Drivers of Tutor Time

on the school's agenda. Student voice is also the time in an academic tutorial (non tutor time) when a tutor, tutee and parents review learning for *as long as it takes* to discuss learning strategies and plot ways forward.

What goes on in tutor time is the building of secure and creative support structures but the mechanisms and skills used are as wide ranging as the tutors involved. The whole of Year 10 and 11 and not just the few, are trained to be mentors and leaders so that they can be the good citizen role models we need them to be. People do not just get placed into tutor groups, they are also prepared. Some may even be trained to deliver support programmes because they are brilliant teachers as well. The tutor will never have to say the words, *'Could you be quiet, please, I want to take the register!'*

Tutor Activity and Drivers (briefly):

1. **The Academic Calendar:** this signals key activities such as Mock Examinations or SATs that tell the tutor who needs support and how. This may be support in T/T with revision. Reports may be looming or academic tutorials and each will spark activity
2. **Assembly:** both Year and House assemblies will be needed. For Year 9 assemblies only the Year 9 kids go, perhaps accompanied by an older student or assistant tutor). The rest stay providing an opportunity for smaller groups. House assemblies mean that everyone goes. Students may well start to lead on House Assemblies adding to a sense of ownership and trust
3. **Heads of House:** these will guide the tutors' work and introduce charity work, competitions, learning ideas and generally engender a sense of belonging and fun supported by a massive rewards for leadership programme. Many ideas will be student driven
4. **Assessment:** Much time will be spent monitoring learning and in supporting learning as needed. The tutor has access to data, direct communication with teacher colleagues and has creative options such as student mentors, LSAs, parents and an Assistant to help out
5. **School Improvement:** the tutor group becomes the perfect body for school feedback, student led, tutor supported with communication direct to staff and the school circumventing the current tedious and low level democracies
6. **Student Voice:** all of this should enrich student voice and make something useful of it that works in line with the school and its values.

The tutor will have many conversations with tutees singly, horizontally and vertically and so will the students both within their mini year groups and with others. Every child will be heard and listened to and everyone will be valued and supported and monitored. The tutees will know that the tutor is in close touch with parents and carers and will constantly monitor student learning but ultimately, the tutee will know that the tutor is their advocate always at their side. When worlds fall apart, the tutor will still be there in the tutee's corner and will always encourage and support. The tutor will give straight answers and will not mistake professionalism with friendship. This nurtures trust and links generations that can share values in a world of flux.

All students are trained and trusted to take on leadership opportunities. Ideas like 'prefects' become philosophically problematic when all are expected to lead. Rewards systems need to be re-thought. The Heads of House (or Community or College) run each House like a school. Each tutor runs a mini-school. All work in self-supporting Teams held by good data and information and by each other to offer fresh insights into learning.

In Fig. 20 below, Heads of College virtually run the whole school through a House or College (or even an 'Abbey') system. The tutor is Head of a mini-school. At last we can reach a stage where the ideals of teachers can be realised. None wanted to work in factory outlets. All wanted to work with young people to make a difference. So we return to Maslow (fig 20 below) and the school journey to self actualisation. This involves not just students but all who work in our schools. Inherent here is the possibility to heal and mend families, improve relationships by listening to stories and by staying positive and creative, supportive and empathic despite the odds.

If the academic calendar signals to the tutor what the priorities are in tutor time in terms of support, it also signals to HOH that they can reinvent and innovate better ways of doing things that involve students rather than being done to students.

Creating Schools within Schools

We can now end our journey into our schools to see if the tutor has transformed. If the school has transformed and the school has understood VT and its values, tutors might say something like this...

'...this is much more fun. At last I understand what tutoring is all about now, especially my role as a mentor and advocate, especially the way I listen, build collaborative partnerships and realise citizenship through tutee leadership. This is exactly what I do in the school and because I do this, the system has started to change around me. I perform that critical role of mentor and advocate that ensures inclusion and it is the kids in my form group who help everyone including those with special needs; they are amazing kids who support me in my work. I cannot believe how quickly I have got to know them all or how they have got to know each other. I replicate the best of family life. Kids really are great teachers, mentors and citizens. I can talk regularly to each tutee about life and learning as individuals, mini-year groups, mixed-age groups and as my vertical tutor group. We are like a family and look after each other and I make regular contact with parents. This is why I came into education; to make a difference. Because of what I do in tutor time and in academic tutorials and wherever I can give support, there is better engagement in learning: the kids seem to mature better and so develop the self-esteem they need to be better learners. It makes me a professional and I feel highly valued. It also makes me a better teacher and everyone else too. Besides, my kids know that I am in direct touch with their teachers who give me the information I need to monitor them! I feel that the school is built around my tutor group. Because the school is like this, and my tutees are all trained to be leaders and mentors, I have a great team and a happy team and feel more in control. Because of what I can do in a vertically tutored school, there is healing and an underpinning of support. It is this that seems to be the key to raising achievement. The system allows me to be 'me' which is who the kids need me to be. Each day starts a new sigmoid curve and is a step up the pyramid of self-esteem.

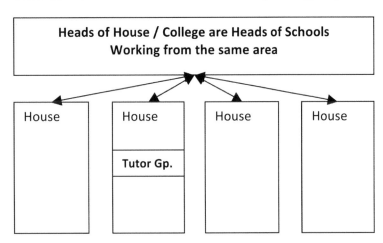

Figure 18: The Basic School Management Structure (Vertical)

It is possible to bring about transformation when we learn that we can be ourselves. The systems we have now prevent the self-actualisation that is at the cloudy top of the Maslow Pyramid.

Management Transformation

Having been a Headteacher / tutor in two mature vertically tutored schools, I can say these things and more! In a vertically tutored school, the absolute key worker (the humble form tutor) operates at the heart of the school next to the student. This is the critical first base of any human scale operation. The Head of Year has become Head of a School House and this too is a transformation from super secretary to super leadership: a management change. The SENCO has become a trainer rather than a pedlar of IEPs. Everyone is now passionate about learning and it is this that makes a school genuinely inclusive. Each House is a small school, each tutor group a mini-school. Macro becomes micro and systems change to suit. Big schools and small schools can be the same. It is process and relationships that make a school great and this has nothing to do with size. Indeed, one of the most outstanding VT comprehensive schools in the country has a population of 2000 most of whom are bussed in. It is high achieving because it innovates and builds relationships that promote great teaching and learning. This is what VT inspires.

In the end, Maslow's Pyramid transforms into a model theory of learning for schools. Vertical Tutoring enables student input to be massively improved in practical, social and psychological terms. Needs are met by good people who are given the opportunity to reform the idea of *'family'* in the school. Social cohesion starts here in the vertical tutor group where care is high quality and built in. At the start of every school year this process begins. In so many schools the opportunity to engage is lost and the tutor abandoned in a pretend system of relationships that rarely holds.

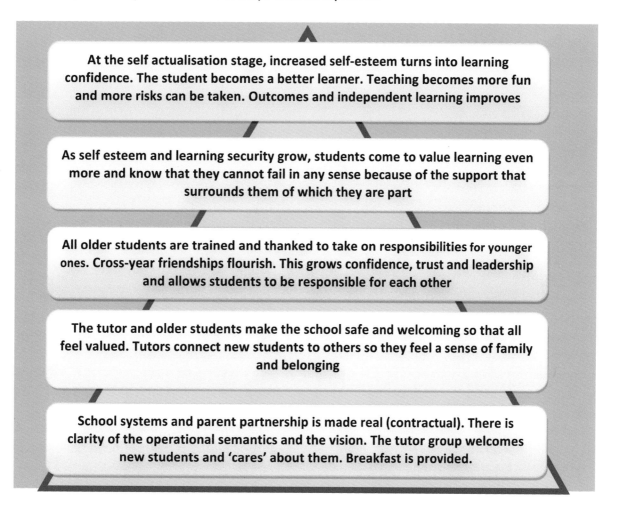

Figure 19: Maslow's Hierarchy of Needs and Vertical Tutoring

VT allows schools to redefine and make sense of *'student voice'*. There are huge manuals written by some LAs on this topic filled with advice, guidance and management initiatives running to hundreds of pages. Invariably, it is the UK top down style to take something simple (listening and valuing) and build it into something complicated that is bureaucratic, unworkable and disparate. We do this because we have to measure, tick a box and cover our backs for when the inspector calls, because that is the system we have built and because we don't really trust teachers or the system. Good people sit in LAs and the DCSF constructing amazing strategies of intricate detail for invisible armies long exhausted by the campaign. For most schools, student voice is a small group elected to meet monthly in the library: such an approach is old hat and requires huge management to be successful and few schools in reality have managed this concept successfully. They still tick the box even though the concept is not really properly thought out and does not work without huge effort!

Yet, within each tutor group is the perfect vehicle for student voice and a return to the idea of 'family', this time extended to embrace both the school and the home. With society and families often under immense pressure such synergy is badly needed. It is this that offers the potential to meet the challenge of social cohesion: the tutor as healer.

Learning Leadership and Management from the Master

The master of Systems Thinking is W. Edwards Deming and the great man has always been one of my personal management guides. I have called heavily on his work throughout this book to put these thoughts down. At this point it is wise to reflect and *'check'* whether any of this book makes management sense. Like Vertical Tutoring, Deming's 14 Point guide for managers of industry has evolved and matured over time and enjoys international respect. These points are adapted here and reinterpreted for schools:

1. **Create constancy of purpose towards improvement:** Aim to develop the learning capability of all students so they can be great bosses and workers and international citizens. Education is for life not for short term targets
2. **Adopt the new philosophy:** Ensure that you really understand Vertical Tutoring by being trained and guided by those few who are expert and have travelled the road. Do not *'incorporate'* VT but leave the past behind without regret and change the school's culture. Evolve by walking the talk of values and Systems Thinking
3. **Cease dependence on inspection to achieve quality:** Build quality and fun into learning. Don't teach to the test or allow inspection to govern what you know to be right. Provide great learning experiences and work with customers. Never waste time preparing for inspection. Compliance is not creative or innovative. Outcomes will improve faster than you thought possible
4. **End the practice of awarding business on the basis of price tag:** Liaise in partnership with feeder schools and tell them what is needed to improve learning quality and so reduce your costs. Invest in them. Form Trusts. This establishes greater loyalty and better customer care. Don't confuse *cost* and *worth*. Mistakes in education are costly and difficult to rectify later on
5. **Improve constantly and forever the system of production and service:** Work with all internal and external customers to improve the service and the process. Build in high quality by innovating and delighting. Establish the front office and the substantive role of the tutor
6. **Institute training on the job:** Make sure everyone gets the training they need including students, staff, parents and governors. Train people in contributing and improving and share what works. Ignore training for compliance and train on the innovative
7. **Institute leadership to help people do better:** Make everyone a leader in the school including students. This raises self-esteem, improves work and helps others. Train students so they can be responsible, help others and be great citizens

8. **Drive out fear so that everyone can work effectively:** fear is now endemic to our schools. It is the duty of Leaders to enable people to do their work well by creating a VT environment where all can work successfully. Fear prevents innovation and increases dependence. People need to be able to speak openly. Cherish your cynics, they were right all along. Remind Unions they are there to make life easier not more difficult and that means understanding school systems not cementing them over

9. **Break down barriers between departments:** Use VT to unite under a learning philosophy that integrates all facets and departments by using the tutor as the conduit. Ensure the end to end process is coherent and checked regularly. Everyone a tutor and teacher. Create a football team and call it 'Pastoral and Academic United'

10. **Eliminate slogans, exhortations and targets for the workforce:** workers in schools do not need to be told that *'every child matters'*. This is adversarial and counterproductive. Implement VT so that every whole child matters. Remember that most mistakes are system errors (94%) and are not the fault of school workers (6%)

11. **Remove barriers that rob workers of the right to be proud of what they do:** Substitute leadership and support for targets and 'measures' of success. Remember teachers and tutors are customers of the school

12. **Abolish appraisal ratings and management by objectives:** targets tend to change behaviours negatively and this is sufficient to make appraisal inappropriate and fearful. Support should be ongoing not annual. Appraisal is not a right but a barrier to joy in work. Bankers all messed up but still got bonuses. Appraisal does not work and it causes cheating! Tell your SIP they should be running their own school better

13. **Institute a vigorous programme of education and self-improvement:** do what it says on the packet and / or get everyone to buy a copy of this book!

14. **The transformation is everybody's job:** everyone in and around the school should be involved in making the change to VT. Make students ambassadors. Ownership is all but external support at the start is essential.

Deming believed that the first step to transformation is the individual. It involves understanding *'profound knowledge'* set out earlier and repeated here.

- ∞ Appreciation for a system
- ∞ Knowledge about variation
- ∞ Theory of knowledge
- ∞ Psychology

If the individual can get to grips with these and understand what each entails and how they are linked, the individual is transformed and ***'will perceive new meaning to his life, to events, to numbers, to interactions between people'.*** Only then is the leader capable of managing and leading the transformation process. Once transformed, says Deming, the individual will

- ∞ **Set an example**
- ∞ **Be a good listener, but will not compromise**
- ∞ **Continually teach other people**
- ∞ **Help people to pull away from their current practice and beliefs and move into the new philosophy without a feeling of guilt about the past**

To effect successful school transformation, the Leadership Team and Headteacher must transform first and this means they must understand the system of Vertical Tutoring at a deep level. Superficial

training and copying other schools is not sufficient. Without this most schools that move to vertical groups will not transform. They cannot let go of old culture, fail to recognise values and compromise rather than lead. Each compromise diminishes people and learning.

When schools ask for support and advice they invariably expect me to train the tutors and can never understand why it is the LT that need to be first up.

I want to leave readers with one final model of a working school. This is the VT Model and is aligned with Systems Thinking and driven by people passionate about learning. We return to the Values Driven School at long last and one that needs no centralist prescription.

The purpose of the school (fig. 20) is to maximise individual human potential, academically and socially, to prepare for the next stage of their journey to international citizenship. Teaching and learning is the process whereby this is achieved and takes place in three critical areas: the family, the tutor group (and House) and the classroom. All three groups must build in value to the process and work seamlessly together especially in the way they manage variation. Back Office resources are tidied up and drawn down to the Front Office and designed around an enhanced tutor role. Over 90% of all school employees are tutors ensuring systems knowledge and understanding. The model sees each group as teachers and mentors / customers and service providers, all managing variation

The messages of Systems Thinking (what Vertical Tutoring demands)

1. **For leadership to be an 'engine of change', the Head becomes a tutor at least for a while. Remember there is a sign above the Head's door, *'No useful work gets done here'*. Understanding the work being done means doing the work and talking to those doing the work (modelling learning). The Leader must design the process; the managers impact on the system (in particular by working in classrooms)**

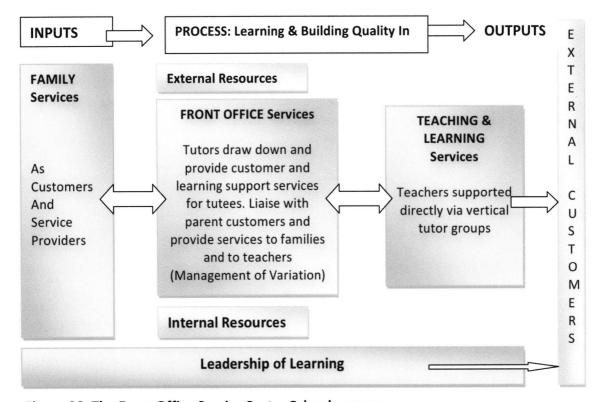

Figure 20: The Front Office Service Sector School: process

2. Schools must work closely with parents by reinstituting the Front Office. Back Office resources are tidied up by Heads of Schools (HOHs). Ask again what prevents the school from being world-class. Remove anything that gets in the way of the process and the freedom of teachers and tutors to work effectively and creatively (with joy). Do everything possible to support front line tutor work. This improves teaching and learning faster and safer

3. Look at the information and data you need especially parent input and staff comments. Manage variation with style and learn from it by talking and listening to customers and suppliers. Work on the theory. Match these with human resource help especially from student leaders in TGs (tutor groups)

4. Keep improving the process so that learning is continuous and personal and built on a foundation of strong learning relationships that improve teaching and learning through innovation and creativity

5. Remember that VT works by building self esteem through leadership and responsibility. This builds a better attitude to learning and makes greater sense of teaching. The Gateways and Deeps support the learning relationship process.

Chapter 15: Concluding Remarks

The School Whisperer

It is easy to read such a list of loose principles (Annexe 1) and the practices described above and to hear good people say, 'We already do that'. In fact, there are only a minority of schools in the country that have changed their culture to truly develop humane learning relationships (process) and more bespoke curriculum practices. However, the number is growing. They are our beautiful butterflies and such schools simply fly and are a delight to watch. For too long, a tick box mentality has denied good Headship and gravely damaged good schools and the development of teaching and learning. Somehow, values, principles, leadership and learning have to combine in a new way and this is what vertical tutoring and its inherent culture can do. Vertical Tutoring cannot be simply mixing up the kids so that the naughty ones are separated out although this is always a good start!

The Dog Whisperer, Cesar Millan, has got it spot on! To create a balanced pack (tutor group) requires a confident pack leader (tutor). You must then ensure that all dogs are given exercise (allowed to talk to each other and be who they are), discipline (training in leadership and responsibility) and rewards in that order. The School Whisperer says much the same. Create balanced tutor groups. Grow great tutors by building school systems that support their leadership and the magic they must perform. Promote leadership in other pack leaders (parents and older students). Exercise values regularly through assertive mentoring relationships. Encourage, build confidence, engender trust and raise self-esteem. Reward good behaviour. Build the management system and learning process needed to support this activity. Create schools within schools, groups within groups so that the conveyor belt is replaced by human scale family groups of front-office learning relationships as the building block of the learning process.

Ultimately, Vertical Tutoring demands that everything in the school has to change over time. Vertical Tutoring is a journey and re-exploration of human scale learning systems: learning systems as opposed to just teaching systems. Lesley Kuhn (2009) puts it this way: 'Thoughtfulness matters in a society dominated by organisational life. Most people work for large organisations for much of their waking hours. Employment in organisations where the leaders or management demand certain responses, and where in order to stay 'safe' employees must respond accordingly, has implications for the sorts of habits of thought that develop. The habits of thought give shape to the kinds of society we inhabit. We need to separate learning to be wise (thoughtful) from learning to be wily (surviving in an organisational setting) for without this the future of civil society is in jeopardy.

Conclusions are all about wise words but I don't really have any. My destiny, so I thought, was to play cricket for Hampshire but I was never good enough. I drifted into teaching and became a Headteacher. Forty years later, I still know that when I go into a school I am in the company of saints, the kind of people who compensated for all my weaknesses and who allowed this maverick to play with systems. The kids still make me laugh and remind me of what it is to have hope and be alive. (I am at least hopeful). When I get home and stare at my computer screen, I despair at the well meaning fools that *run* education and their pontificating about system improvements, reforms and their critical judgements on people who sacrifice so much for others. They are old culture politicians preaching about the knowledge society they effectively undermine. They are a barrier to the future not a Gateway. *'Those who do the job know best...'*

The journey across *'The Sea of Better Schools'* and through the mysterious and misty passes of *'the 'Key Stage Mountains'* is one that all schools must make; it is exciting but can be dangerous. The geography is constantly changing, and steering a safe improvement course is not easy in a world where signposts change overnight. To do this successfully requires all travellers, tutors, teachers, governors, students, support staff, and parents to work together and contribute what information each has to make the front office effective. Each supports the other, everyone a teacher, everyone a learner, each providing services to the other in the school's information and learning market. The school ensures that the form tutor is at the organisational hub of such a synergy because there is no alternative. You build from the base up not from the top down. Partnerships have to be real otherwise there is no moral purpose.

Goleman (1995) introduced us to the world of emotional intelligence. Emotional intelligence involves understanding what makes people tick and give of their best. The various traits are grouped as follows with group 1 being the starting point; the last dependent on the other three. It is the stuff of leadership. This has everything to do with understanding Vertical Tutoring, service provision, organisational awareness and teams.

Table 10: Emotional Intelligence in Leadership

1. **Self Awareness**	2. **Other Awareness**
Emotional self-awareness and self assessment (know thyself)	Empathy; organisational awareness; serve orientation (leader as Servant)
3. **Self Management**	4. **Social Skills**
Self control; trustworthiness	Teamwork; collaboration

In some ways the journey from where schools are now to a culture of Vertical Tutoring is a no brainer! Nothing could be simpler, so why do managers have such difficulty with transformation and turning their schools into butterflies and enjoying at least a breath of freedom? It has much to do with the long term damage of prescription, fear and centralist ideology. Such a journey should have a spiritual quality more than anything else because learning is the most important journey of all. VT is the next stage of where schools need to be. It is therefore an epic journey from IQ (intelligence) to EQ (emotional intelligence) and on to SQ (spiritual intelligence). It is, in fact, a journey back to where we started. SQ is built from the same creative chaos as quantum mechanics: it transforms, innovates and recreates. Extended families (tutor front office), village communities (the tutor group and school) and the concept of *'the whole child'* all linked in a real partnership process through the creative chaos of learning and the management challenge of variation.

Danar Zohars (1999) described the spiritual quality of organisations in the following terms. It is a heady mix of Quantum Theory, organisational principles, Systems Thinking and values. Like Kuhn, Zohars embraces chaos and Bertalanffy's understanding of *active personality systems* and the delight in the natural order of chaos; of *disequilibrium*. Teachers understand this.

- ∞ Be flexible; (beware of compliance to old systems; be prepared to unlearn)
- ∞ Be self-aware: live with space and silence (be yourself)
- ∞ Be holistic: see the bigger picture: (stand back and re-evaluate)
- ∞ Have a vision: be led by your values (always)
- ∞ Be open to diversity: learn from death and failure
- ∞ Stand out against the crowd: be a Good Samaritan
- ∞ Be open to diversity: reframe - step back
- ∞ Advance to the edge: be a little uncomfortable

Schools will understand how to interpret such a view of spiritual intelligence and so develop into the magical and heroic places that we need them to be and which most are. The great educationist, writer and School Principal, Theodore Sizer (1984) put it this way:

'Inspiration, hunger: these are the qualities that drive good schools. The best we educationists can do is create the most likely conditions for them to flourish, and then get out of the way.'

If only governments could do this. If only schools could develop the trust needed. Learning feeds hunger and inspires: however, it can only do these things if systems get out of the way and allow process to develop. To change to a culture of VT, schools must *advance to the edge, be a little uncomfortable*. Students and staff must be Good Samaritans and not be frightened to cross over and help and to embrace the big picture. The risk of cultural change is not taking the risk.

Leadership is not easy and life in a school can be hugely demanding on personnel. There is criticism, blame, fear, loneliness and a constant drain on energy. The responsibilities are enormous. On the bridge of the Star Ship Enterprise, Jean Luc Picard at the start of some epic journey would say those magic words *'Let it be so…engage'*. It is a metaphor as well as a signal for engineering. Not only is warp drive connected to the propulsion unit but people are connected to each other. Indeed, most can only really function when working as a team and feeling supported and valued. This is the essence of vertical tutoring and is the way we are defined and shaped by others. It should be the way we build systems.

In the end it is the karma of western governments for their systems to break down and fail as they try to control the quantum mechanics of complex societies that have lost a combining culture and are in search of what Jimmy Carter called a *'mosaic'*. Systems can never be all things to all people: just as Heads of House must not do the job of form tutors, so governments should not do the job of Headteachers and parents. Again, *'The person doing the job is the person best placed to do the job'.*

We institutionalise compliance with endless controls and regulations in systems that cannot hold. We see this in Headteacher training, teacher trade unions, our National Curriculum, the inspection processes, target setting and then in our school structures and in the way LTs think. We lose our emotional intelligence and cannot realise the spiritual. Centralist systems start out well but over time the systems have to be constantly repaired by introducing more directives, more reforms, more regulation, extra guidance, laws and prescription. As control increases, democracy retreats. In the end, adding new parts to old simply stores up trouble for the future and the hollowing out of government merely serves to deflect and dissipate system incompetence on those least responsible, our teachers. We end up with new bits bolted on to broken bits and call it *'reform'* and the whole structure totters, and the first to fall are always the most vulnerable. It is ironic that centralism relies on the innovation and creativity it stifles. Chaos will always escape and vote you out.

It seems that only independent-minded Headteachers and LTs can rescue the situation and create schools that are genuinely values driven and constructed around the whole child.

This book has concentrated on secondary schools, but the system is just as problematic at primary level and more so in Middle Schools. It is there where we see Headship overly dependent on central direction, one of the many SIGGS hypotheses on the centralism/dependency issue (especially Nos. 61, 62, 64 and 66). We sell to kids and to parents the idea of *breadth and balance* and their *entitlement* to access a mythical National Curriculum when many need a more personalised curriculum that first ensures that they can read and write and do sums. Vertical Tutoring simply invites us to look again at the fun that learning can and should be when schools decide direction based on sound values, a workable system process and the security of learning relationships. Vertical Tutoring is complex because it is simple: it is complicated because it is common sense; it is the right path because it heals and brings generations together. It detoxes rather than botoxes organisations.

I have talked much of 'Learning Relationships'. Jonathan Haidt in his excellent book, '*The Happiness Hypothesis*', offers a short conclusion to *the Meaning of Life* and the human condition.

'...Just as plants need sun, water and good soil to thrive, people need love, work and a connection to something larger. It is worth striving to get the right relationships between yourself and others, between yourself and your work, and between yourself and something larger than yourself. If you get these relationships right, a sense of purpose and well-being will emerge.'

Vertical tutoring works to ensure we get the learning relationships right. In many ways, the rider needs to follow the elephant, occasionally guiding it along: it is older and has its own wisdom based on its capacity to learn. Our teachers, tutors, governors and school workers have amazing talent. It is my joy to travel with them when invited to do so, and to share their good company. They remain the last of the altruistic, professional volunteers and can yet be our world class teacher heroes. In my book, they already are.

Peter A Barnard

April 2010

Postscript

This book was completed before the General Election of 2010. A postscript is needed.

The first decade of the new millennium has been one of massive centralist intervention sold to schools as partnership. The damage to leadership, learning and systems has been immense. When a culture of dependency and compliance is created, thinking outside of any box becomes almost impossible. The real problem, however, is knowing you are in a box. Our new political masters have their work cut out. They too must let go of the past and trust schools to do the work. They must cut the apron strings and release the good chaos that can best switch the aspiration gene back on. Schools have a decision to make. It is the 'academy' decision in essence. It is schools working with parents that must lead communities and build partnerships that serve their front office learning services. This is different from the systems we have and requires new leadership. At the base of the system are vertical systems and learning relationships. Everyone a teacher, everyone a learner. Only then can every child matter.

Principles:

The key changes, themes and inherent principles of Vertical Tutoring:

These were written way back: they are included here as an overview; conscious that we seem to live in a world of 'enhancements'!

1. Enhance Human Relationships

Vertical Tutoring is actually about Schools as Organisations and the way schools operate. It is a means of changing the organisational culture of schools into what they always wanted to be: places where learning is centrally placed and where all stakeholders (students, staff, parents and the wider community) can contribute more equally to the learning and support processes. It is in fact a contribution to Systems Thinking and the philosophy of organisations which places people at the heart of all decisions and where the ownership of learning is better shared. The principle here is to ensure that all partners involved in learning play their part. This changes the way the school operates and reveals current 'partnerships' to be superficial and even negative. Vertical Tutoring ensures that students have time and support to be the citizens we need them to be by ensuring that they are an integral part of the communications conduit and are valued for their input (co-construction). At the heart of all organisations are conversations between creative people. Vertical Tutoring as a concept attempts to encourage, capture and nurture these 'affective learning relationships' and build new management structures around them (transformation) that effectively changes macro bureaucracies into micro systems. Contained in these relationships is the notion that schools can greatly support family life, raise self-esteem and ensure that every child matters.

2. Enhance Creative Use of Data and Information:

Variation prevents quality from being built into processes so its management is critical. Learning is informed by data and information. Data is comparative and statistical in form and requires other information sources from parents, teachers and others to be effective and to make sure that there is the best possible oversight and support for 'the whole' child. Data on its own is deeply flawed and can alienate students and parents (undermine quality). Vertical Tutoring without good data and information capture misses the organisational and operational point of partnership. Learning conversations raise important questions about data and place high value on parent, student and tutor input. That discussion ('deep' conversation or academic tutorial) uses data creatively to better plan the learning process and the learning journey. Parents and students have stories to tell and VT ensures that time is invested to listen (manage variation). Information lights the way forward. This is the real heart of 'student voice'. Data is not a series of numbers and letters but must include stories of learning and full teacher comments so that the right questions can be asked and good answers sought. Without these, there is no humanity in the learning relationships we need. This establishes an information market around 'front offices' and new (transformational) management support structures.

3. Enhance Personal Curriculum:

It is the discussion between the many voices involved in the learning processes, including subject teachers, tutors, students and parents which should define and shape a more personalised curriculum and allow individual human potential (not just that of the student but of staff and parents too) to develop. It is the many stories of the many journeys by so many students and their parents that should be the main drivers of learning. This is why the National Curriculum must be allowed to fade, having done its job of kick-starting a culture of education that had grown moribund. However, schools must listen to parental and student learning stories and be able to respond. It is these stories of learning that should inspire curriculum development alongside a national learning and achievement framework. Again, there is a need to transform management as learning rightly becomes more bespoke. The notion of 'breadth and balance' was always a strange idea as was the falsehood of 'entitlement': both need individualised definition. However, it begins with teaching kids to read and do sums over and above any access to some perceived curriculum programme.

4. Enhance Teaching and Learning

VT and Systems Thinking indicate that our current view of teaching and learning has become narrowly focused around the classroom. Teachers have been isolated from the system and have been wrongly led to believe that their performance and student outcomes are entirely down to them. Parents, tutors, other students and staff are all teachers and all have a responsibility for performance. A VT school changes the culture by ensuring that learning is an operational process that recognises and supports all of the characters involved. It joins the school up by establishing the importance of 'front office' thinking and the critical role of tutor, parents and peers. By re-gearing the organisation, students feel more equipped to engage in learning and teaching is better facilitated and improves. As things stand teachers face the challenge of building learning relationships against a background of time pressure, coverage and support systems that are upside down.

5. Enhance Care

There was never a time when 'every child did not matter!' What has been at fault was a 'soft' and simplistic view of care (pastoral) in schools that is too often separated from learning; a safety net to catch those who fall. Vertical Tutoring seeks to redefine 'care' in a deeper sense. It goes beyond ECM and bolt-on structural fixes. VT ensures that the wider 'village' sees care holistically and especially in support for learning. Effectively, pastoral and academic bureaucracies are replaced by a learning synergy whereby deep care is implicit. To do this the tutor must return to being an active advocate and mentor. Learning and care in a vertically tutored school go hand in hand. Indeed all descriptors move from abused semantics and assumptions to reality, and this too should transform management.

6. Enhance Leadership

Growing leaders in school is an essential activity. Paradoxically, if we concentrated far more on providing endless leadership opportunities for students, improved staff leadership would automatically follow. Thus, 'Citizenship' was never a 'subject' to be studied as such but is in essence, the way we run our schools and the way we care for and involve each other and help each other make good decisions. Leadership, almost by definition, is best developed in the safety of mixed-age groups that some call 'family', and vertical groupings greatly enhance leadership opportunities and trust as core human values.

All students have to be given leadership opportunities and training to provide confidence and raise self-esteem. This leads to greater empathy, reciprocity and those virtues that improve engagement with learning, in order that they become the citizens that we need them to be and they want to be. Headship training is in urgent need of an overhaul. At the moment Heads are leading schools by compliance and are unable to innovate. This is a management and systems issue first, not a vision issue.

7. Enhance Student Voice

Our view of 'student voice' is hugely constrained in horizontal systems because organisational thinking is so inconsiderate and bureaucratic. We need to move beyond councils and the representative voice, right and proper though these may appear to be, to hearing every student's voice. In essence, we must broaden the concept so that each individual voice is heard. Even that is not enough. Parents too need to be heard and to be engaged in the deep conversations that our complex and fast moving society ignores. Vertical Tutoring nurtures and ensures such engagement that encourages the conversations, that listens to the voices, that enables the organisation to respond. It is a virtuous circle. All voices are heard but this can only happen when time is re-invested in people. From a simple conversation, we need to re-grow and re-nurture student voice and this too transforms management. Each vertical tutor group is a perfect school council. Rather than see Student Voice as a separate representative system, it might be better developed as one that is integrated into the learning process but this means VT must be properly implemented first.

8. Enhance the Academic Tutorial

At the heart of Vertical Tutoring is the Academic Tutorial or Deep Learning Conversation. This is when the tutor (the school) meets with parents and the tutee at a critical learning time with all the relevant information (full school report) there. It is an investment in people unrestricted by bells and time constraints. Vertical tutoring without the full academic tutorials misses the whole point completely and fails students, parents and staff. It is the key that releases and enhances learning if done properly. Some schools claim to do this in a closure day with tutors seeing parents and students for 10/15 minutes one after the other. This may be better than nothing but it falls dangerously short of what is needed. It also has the potential to be hugely damaging to staff and to student/parent engagement. The academic tutorial time has no time restraints in a truly vertical system because the academic calendar spreads the engagement load over the year. It is this single act at critical learning times that is the single most important conversation in the school year. It is deep, reflective, positive and even spiritual and very much life-enhancing and learner friendly. This too transforms management, and schools omit this at great cost.

9. Enhance 'Family'

For a child, to be an important member of a mixed age group (where all are engaged in support, mentoring and leadership at various times) has to be sensible in an age when the family, in so many cases, is in crisis or under pressure and society, toxic. It is natural for older students to take the responsibilities we invariably deny them in horizontal systems. VT also allows the tutor to be a healer and help families by supporting them through tough times using the improved communication VT offers. Students are also members of Houses and the community beyond. In family type groups, the tutors can facilitate a place for everyone. It is simply safer, more natural and more fun. It is also more 'educational' and more achievement orientated and learner friendly. Of course, the demands on the tutor increase but only because of the need to 'unlearn' one system and engage with a more natural, relaxed and professional style. The tutor is head of family in school and needs to be the person kids need him/her to be. It was always that way but somehow got lost. Perhaps this is the real antidote to the gang and to rising levels of childhood anxiety.

10. Enhance Chaos

I wrote about this many years ago in 'Chaos, Culture and Third Millennium Schools' (still an excellent read!). Like quantum mechanics, learning and human relationships are complex and can form and reform in an instant. The system we currently have is all about control, regulation and targets which changes behaviour for the worse. It stultifies and dulls the spirit and can never capture creative learning because learning is human and chaotic. VT recognises the chaos of learning relationships as being creative, fun, full of change and rich in information. The skill is to use, and to make sense of chaos and innovate around it. VT creates operational systems that welcome and thrive on the challenges of learning. All of these principles above are elementally chaotic and therefore present an unexplored territory for those Headteacher prophets and leaders at home in a land without signposts.

Bibliography:

Barnard, P. (2000). *Chaos, Culture and Third Millennium Schools'*: Apocalypse Press, Guildford, Surrey, UK

Belbin, R. M. (1996). *The Coming shape of Organisation:* Butterworth Heinemann; Oxford

Bertalanffy, Ludwig von (1968). *General System Theory: Foundations, Development, Applications'* (1968): George Braziller, NY. Revised Edition, 1976

Brighouse, T. (2008). *Education without Failure*: article in RSA Journal, Autumn (2008): London

Bruner, J. (1963). *The Process of Education*: A Reader's Journal: Harvard University Press, Cambridge, Ma

Cambridge Report into Primary Education: Robin Alexander, Editor (2009). *Children, their World, their Education:* Routledge

Carnie, F. (2004). *Pathways to Child Friendly Schools*: Human Scale Education

Clegg, B. & Birch, P. (1998). *Disorganisation*: Financial Times; Pitman Publishing, London

Deming, W. Edwards (1982). *Out of the Crisis*: MIT (Ma)

Druker, P. (1994). Abstracted from Beatty, J. (1998). *The World According to Druker:* Ch. 8. The Orion Publishing Group, London

Durkheim E. (1952). *Suicide.* J. A. Spalding & G. Simpson, Trans. New York: Free Press

Epstein, J. Levy (1995). *School/Family/Community: Caring for the Children we Share:* Phi Delta Kappan; v. 76 May 1995 pp 701-12. See also, Epstein, J, levy (2001). *School Family and Community: Preparing Educators and Improving Schools:* Boulder CO, Westview Press

Goleman, D. (1995). *Emotional Intelligence:* Bantam Books, NY

Haidt, J. (2006). *The Happiness Hypothesis*: Arrow Books, London

Haidt, J. & Joseph, C (2007). *The Moral Mind: how five sets of innate moral intuitions guide the development of many culture-specific virtues and modules* in Carruthers, P., Laurence, S. & Stich, S. [editors] (2007). *The Innate mind*: Vol. 3. NY / Oxford pp. 367-391

Handy, C. (1989). *The Age of Unreason*: Business Books Ltd., London. See also

Handy, C. (1994). *The Empty Raincoat*: Hutchinson, London and

Handy, C. (1998). *The Hungry Spirit*: Hutchinson, London

Hargreaves, D. H. (2006). *A New Shape for Schooling?* SSAT, Milbank, London

Huizinga, J. (1938). *Homo Ludens:* Gelden Literary Agency, NL

Johnston, R. & Clark, G. (2001). *Service Operations Management*: Pearson Education Ltd., Harlow

Kanter, R. M. (1998). *When Giants Learn to Dance*: International Thompson Business Press, London

King, K. & Frick, T. (1999). *Systems Thinking: The Key to Educational Redesign.* Paper presented at the annual meeting of the American Educational Research Association April 19, 1999, Montreal, Canada

Kuhn, L. (2009). *Adventures in Complexity: for Organisations near the Edge of Chaos*: Triarchy Press, Devon. See also, Lakoff, G. (1987). Women, *Fire and Dangerous Things: What Categories Reveal about the Mind*: Chicago, University of Chicago Press

Langford, D. P. & Cleary, B. A. (1995). *Orchestrating Learning with Quality:* ASQC Quality Press, Milwaukee, Wisconsin

Maccia E. & Maccia G. (1996). *'Development of educational theory derived from three models'* (1966): Washington DC: US Office of Education; Project no. 5-0368. See also *SIGGS Theory Model'* (1966) updated by T W Frigg 1996 (web)

Marcus, G. (2004). *The Birth of the Mind*: Basic Books. NY

McCrae, R. R. (1996): *Social Consequences of Experiential Openness:* Psychological Bulletin, 120; pp 323-337. See also, McCrae, R. & Sutin, A. R. (1996). *Openness to Experience:* in **Leary, M. R. and Hoyle, R. H**. (2009) *Handbook of Individual Differences in Social Behaviour*; Guilford Press, NY. See also, McCrae, R. R. & Costa, P.T., Jr. (2007). *Personality Trait Structure as a Human Universal*: American Psychologist, 52. 1997 and *'Toward a new generation of personality theories'* (2006): In J. S. Wiggins (Ed.), *The five-factor model of personality: Theoretical perspectives* (pp. 51-87) New York: Guilford.

McKinsey Report (2007). *How the World's Best Performing Schools Come Out on Top'*: published on McKinsey website

Nathan, L. (2010). *The Hardest Questions Aren't on the Test*: Beacon Press, Boston

Orwell, G. (1945). *Animal Farm: A Fairy Story:* Penguin Group, London

Palmer, S. (2006). *Toxic Childhood:* Orion, London

Pinker, S. (2002). *The Blank Slate*: Penguin Group, London

Rankin, B. (2004). *The Importance of Intentional Socialisation Among Children in Small Groups*: Early Childhood Education Journal; Vol. 32, No. 2 pp 81-85

Rowling, J. K. (1997). *Harry Potter and the Sorcerer's Stone*: Bloomsbury, London

Schratz, M. (2008). *Review of McKinsey Report'*: Journal of Educational Change; 9: 321-324; Springer, Netherlands

Sizer, T. R. (1984 & 1992). *Horace's Compromise*: Houghton Mifflin, Boston, Ma. See also, Sizer, T. R. (1996). *Horace's School: Redesigning the American High school:* Houghton Mifflin, Boston, Ma

Seddon, J. (2008). *Systems Thinking in the Public Sector*: Triarchy Press, Devon, UK. See also,

Senge, P. (1993). *The Fifth Discipline: the art and practice of the learning organisation*: Doubleday, US; Century Business, UK

Shukla, M. (1994). *Why Corporations Fail*: published in Productivity 34(4), pp 629-639 and on the web

Sizer, T. (1984 and 1992). *Horace's Compromise: The Dilemma of the American High School:* Houghton Miflin, Boston

Steiner, R. (1995). *Kingdom of Childhood*: Anthroposophic Press, NY

Sternberg, R. J. (1998), *A Balance Theory of Wisdom*: Review of General Psychology, 2, 347-365. Discussed in Haidt, J. (2006). *The Happiness Hypothesis:* pp 152-153; Arrow Books, London

Zohars, D. (1999). *Spiritual Intelligence- the Ultimate Intelligence*: Bloomsbury Corp, London

Figure

Figure 1 (p 10): The problem for schools here is that *checking* the system cannot be easily done. It is assumed that horizontal structures are benign and that common practice across schools, especially at the point of student entry, is OK. So many assumptions lead to a semi-rationalised view of school operations, and learning relationships as a systems process become confused.

Table 1 (p 11): This adapted Table contains the differentials between horizontal and vertical systems. Key emphasis here is the wrong idea that managers manage people first rather than systems. If the system is right, people (teachers) tend to be effective, responsible and self-accountable. This is why teachers are seen as problematic by governments rather than the systems in which they work. The last New Labour regime to 2010, of big government, has been the classic command and control model and has failed miserably. Systems thinking emphasises the individual and the successful management of variation.

Figure 2 (p 15): This typical school model is misleading from a Systems Thinking perspective. It is true that what happens in the classroom is of the highest importance *but* there is a big BUT. This causes a system to grow whereby the pastoral side is seen as either a repair shop for broken kids or a safety blanket for system *victims.* Systems Thinking says that it is the pastoral system that actually undermines teaching and learning through the **kind of induction rituals** across virtually all schools.

Figure 3 (p 19): Figure 3 adjusts the process of support. Here the back office system which schools have and which the last government has built at high expense is realigned into a front office system. The tutor role becomes highly significant and high status and is serviced by support teams. This enables the tutor to ensure that students are ready to go to the classroom and supported directly. This also changes significantly the perception of staff in the eyes of students to one of high status.

Figure 4 (p 22): The model that has developed is one that has damaged the critical relationship between schools and families (parents). There is no school/parent partnership; in fact the New Labour government not only undermined this idea but used parents and *rights* as a means to control *errant* schools and teachers. All organisations need to work closely and directly with customers. Vertical Tutoring addresses this directly and permanently.

Table 2 (p 30): Research into VT is extremely limited which is good. It keeps VT *clean* philosophically. Most research has badly damaged education by confusing systems assumptions and common sense. If thousands of school teachers believe parents and students are very powerful influences on learning, any system schools use to support learning must embrace the idea that parents and students are also teachers. Student Voice is not an answer in the form that it is conceptually. VT shows how to incorporate key players in a front office synergy.

Figure 5 (p 38): This table illustrates the extent of current back office bureaucratic confusion dressed up as workforce reform. It is in fact an illustration of why Hargreaves' *nine gateways* don't quite lead to the *four deeps.* Workforce reform has simply propped up back offices rather than a newly formed front office system. Such attempts create bad chaos rather than use chaos creatively.

Table 3 (p 40): The idea of *the Deeps* is important but can only work effectively in Vertical Tutoring. To buy into this notion without changing the learning operational process / system does not work effectively and simply assumes transformation.

Figure 6 (p 46): Figure 6 sets out the basic back office system that schools use. What seems coherent is actually unworkable without a massive workforce increase. Even then teaching and learning is actually undermined by presenting young people as social victims. Schools have inadvertently taken this further and actually created education process *victims* and an organisational feedback loop that has distorted operational effectiveness.

Figure 7 (p 49): In fact there are three areas that drive school improvement and it is only when we create schools (VT schools) that understand these drivers that we can really look at pedagogy and teaching and learning issues. These are Psychology, Customer Services and Systems Thinking. Together they combine coherent learning relationships that determine the tutor role and the way we design schools.

Table 4 (p 50): Belbin's ideas have always been helpful in securing a better understanding or organisational systems. It is always worth asking why UK systems seem to fail in such catastrophic ways. They then get rebuilt by people who have never worked in the system and who assume that all component parts (rewards, training, employees, time etc) are non-problematic.

Table 5 (p 51): Of course insects in hives and nests are invariably relatives of each other. In this table, I have tried to show that schools can adapt and learn from insects. Unless we change, we damage parenting and tutors and undermine teaching and learning. In effect, we tend to switch off the aspiration gene rather than switch it on!

Table 6 (p 65): This table is important. It is possible to be arrogant and ignorant and a great Headteacher all at the same time. Some Heads can make bad systems appear to work and this confuses everyone! They are of course in denial and are unable to make the transformational shift necessary or identify that they are stuck in a box. These same people are likely to make a mess of VT because their personality traits and high ability bring us back to the sins of arrogance and ignorance.

Table 7 (p 67): This table adapts Shukla's observations to schools. It provides a good platform to think about schools and how they operate and, indeed, training issues for Headteachers via the NPQH which seems to me to be inadequate (*compliance to a system that doesn't work*). This table applies to good schools as well as those that are struggling.

Figure 8 (p 68): I learned more about schools from Charles Handy than any writer on education. In The Empty Raincoat, Handy introduced us to the 'S' curve as a metaphor for products and organisations. It is adapted here for schools and first appeared in my Chaos, Culture book in 2000. It is a combining picture of organisational development and states that change is ongoing but understanding that the curve identifies the key time to change (point A).

Figure 9 (p 73): At last, the secular psychology of Maslow reminds us of what schools are all about and also tells us (indicates) how they should work. Maslow combined his idea of *peak experiences* and (for me) set out the spiritual nature of organisations and of life (see also Danar Zohar's work). Education is all about producing good people. Our schools believe this but are not yet organised to achieve this. Vertical Tutoring ensures that this is what we do before we engage curriculum... the first learning if you like and the key role of tutor and parent.

Figure 10 (p 80): There is an assumed model and a working model and both are the same. In horizontal year systems, the tutor is rendered ineffective, the parent largely ignored and the teacher undermined. Students pick up on this failing. VT shows how this same model can be made to work properly and students re-engaged.

Figure 11 (p 81): The key here is the AT (Academic Tutorial) or Deep Learning Conversation. This meeting between child, tutor and parent brings together all the data (social and academic) needed to support learning and to show that the school *cares*. It does this at critical times and is not time restricted. Only in VT can this be done.

Figure 12 (p 84): Here learning is part of a process. The family engage direct with the tutor who is the gatekeeper to the school as an organisation. (S)he draws down and enables access to learning and is the main conduit to the human resources needed. In this model, all are effective, engaged and valued.

Figure 13 (p 89): Schools should be seen as information markets capable of managing variation. It is a complete model of information and services that is built around the learner rather like a village community or extended family. It is, in essence, the VT Model.

Figure 14 (p 91): In this service model, everyone gives and receives services. There are no exceptions. Once this is working well, other external services feed into the system so that everything works as a learning process and everyone knows what their role is and the contribution that role makes.

Figure 15 (p 92): Here, we start to identify the nature of transformation as everybody involved in the learning process starts to work operationally in a coherent and synergetic way.

Figure 16 (p 93): In Figure 16, front office services take over (or make sense of) back office service systems. The tutor takes the pivotal role in maintaining and building learning support services working alongside the tutee. This is very different to how schools work though many think this is what they do!

Table 8 (p 95): Transformation has been set against Roz Kanter's work which is always useful especially when dealing with change. She, like Haidt, uses elephants (this time dancing ones) as a metaphor. Again, her table is adapted to show the human nature of school transformation.

Table 9 (p 96): This is a checklist of transformational changes as schools move from a horizontal to a vertical organisational culture. This is where creativity and chaos become synergetic and learning more fun. Item 2 is a paradox; can you figure out why? The answer is that to manage a horizontal tutor group requires astonishing teaching skill and time.

Figure 17 (p 102): Not surprisingly, schools and tutors worry about vertical groups and change. The main activity in tutor time is conversations. This is not a time to deliver programmes but to support learning. It is *SEAL* in many ways. In fact, this activity, if correctly introduced, is easy. If wrongly introduced or seen as an opportunity to deliver PSHE programmes and to impress Ofsted, it is wrong and misunderstood (more compliance and old culture)!

Figure 18 (p 104): The key here is the creation of the Heads of House into a team that works from the same physical base within a student support area. The second is the idea of the tutor as Head of his mini-school. It is the tutor who is the Head of Learning and assessment and the Head of House or College who manages the system and ensure all is working well and any gaps plugged. Schools often have these the wrong way round especially in year systems. This also explains why the US system of counsellors is a deficit model.

Figure 19 (p 105): This figure interprets Maslow's Hierarchy with respect to VT. There appears to be an excellent correlation between the two. The pyramid indicates how schools are managed and works under the banner of learning relationships.

Figure 20 (p 108): The original model (above) has been turned sideways to show learning as a journey and process. Here the school is organisationally coherent with all partnerships in place and contributing to learning as a process.

Table 10 (p 111): During school training I try to show how VT is a journey from IQ to EQ and to SQ (spiritual intelligence). The Emotional Intelligence section deserves more time especially within the area of organisations and leadership. This correlates well with the earlier work of Deming set out later but thematic to this book.

To Laurent, Patricia and Smudge the Cat

UKIC010450200313
207913UK00006B